More Praise for *Be the Best Bad Presenter Ever*

"*Be the Best Bad Presenter Ever* is my second favorite book on public speaking!"

—Malcolm Kushner, author of *Public Speaking for Dummies*

"Public speaking is the #1 fear of almost everyone. People are more afraid of speaking to a group than they are of snakes, spiders, or even burglars. But fear no more! Karen Hough's new book shows you how to feel your fear and do it anyway. Learn how to fumble, stumble, or even forget your lines—but still deliver a killer presentation!"

—BJ Gallagher, coauthor of *A Peacock in the Land of Penguins*

"Karen's book just makes me want to get out there and do it. Be yourself and damn the torpedoes! How refreshing."

—Rick Gilbert, author of *Speaking Up*

BE THE BEST BAD PRESENTER EVER

Also by Karen Hough

*The Improvisation Edge: Secrets to Building
Trust and Radical Collaboration at Work*

*The ImprovEdge Everyday Coaching Model:
Handling Tough Conversations in Three Simple Steps*

Yes! Deck

BE THE
BEST
BAD PRESENTER
EVER

BREAK THE RULES, MAKE MISTAKES, AND WIN THEM OVER

KAREN HOUGH

Berrett–Koehler Publishers, Inc.
San Francisco
a BK Life book

Berrett-Koehler Publishers, Inc.
235 Montgomery Street, Suite 650, San Francisco, CA 94104-2916
Tel: (415) 288-0260 • Fax: (415) 362-2512 • www.bkconnection.com

ORDERING INFORMATION
QUANTITY SALES. Special discounts are available on quantity purchases by corporations, associations, and others. For details, contact the "Special Sales Department" at the Berrett-Koehler address above.

INDIVIDUAL SALES. Berrett-Koehler publications are available through most bookstores. They can also be ordered directly from Berrett-Koehler: Tel: (800) 929-2929; Fax: (802) 864-7626; www.bkconnection.com

ORDERS FOR COLLEGE TEXTBOOK/COURSE ADOPTION USE. Please contact Berrett-Koehler: Tel: (800) 929-2929; Fax: (802) 864-7626.

ORDERS BY U.S. TRADE BOOKSTORES AND WHOLESALERS. Please contact Ingram Publisher Services, Tel: (800) 509-4887; Fax: (800) 838-1149; E-mail: customer.service@ingrampublisherservices.com; or visit www.ingrampublisherservices.com/Ordering for details about electronic ordering.

Berrett-Koehler and the BK logo are registered trademarks of Berrett-Koehler Publishers, Inc.

Printed in the United States of America

Berrett-Koehler books are printed on long-lasting acid-free paper. When it is available, we choose paper that has been manufactured by environmentally responsible processes. These may include using trees grown in sustainable forests, incorporating recycled paper, minimizing chlorine in bleaching, or recycling the energy produced at the paper mill.

LIBRARY OF CONGRESS CATALOGING-IN-PUBLICATION DATA
Hough, Karen.
Be the best bad presenter ever : break the rules, make mistakes, and win them over / Karen Hough.
  pages   cm
ISBN 978-1-62656-047-5 (pbk.)
1. Business presentations. 2. Public speaking. 3. Business communication. I. Title.
HF5718.22.H68 2014
658.4'52—dc23

2014002744

FIRST EDITION

19 18 17 16 15 14   10 9 8 7 6 5 4 3 2 1

Cover design: Irene Morris Design. Project management and interior design: VJB/Scribe. Copyediting: John Pierce. Proofreading: Don Roberts. Index: George Draffan. Illustrations: Jeevan Sivasubramaniam and Jeremy Sullivan. Author photo: R. Gust Smith.

To Mom and Dad
who enthusiastically attended every speech, performance, and
improvisation—no matter how "bad" or bad it was.

CONTENTS

THREE

OOPS!

Staying Bad, No Matter What Happens   107

Break These Rules

Now Get Out There!   131

SO WHO SAID YOU'RE A "BAD" PRESENTER?

Respected Rules for Speaking and Why You Should Break Them—Mercilessly

Let me guess: You're a terrible presenter, right? You hate giving presentations. Some teacher or boss told you that you just don't have it when it comes to presenting. I bet that was a fun day. You'd love never to stand up in front of a crowd again, but you're stuck. You're required to present, maybe because of your job or your position in the community. And every time another presentation comes up, all you can think is "Ugh."

Or maybe you're a pretty decent presenter. You like taking on a challenge, but you sometimes get hung up on all the things you're supposed to do. You feel excited to stand up but still worry that you're not following all the rules.

I bet something else is true, too. You really *do* have something important to say. You've got a few opinions and probably a message you'd love to share with people—if only you could stop shaking and sweating.

So you took all the feedback to heart. You tried to change. First you tried to mimic famous orators or entertainers—and that made you feel like you were wearing someone else's clothes and they didn't fit. Then you took classes, learned the "rules of speaking," and accepted abuse from counselors who just made you feel more awkward and worried. You just can't seem to get what you want, and you hate the fake, sales-y approach—which, of course, makes you hate presenting even more.

Excellent!

You have more potential to give great presentations than any polished phony on the planet. Because guess what? You're *not* innately a terrible presenter. Someone else's rules are making you "bad"—rules from Presentations 101—the rules that box you in, regulate everything you do, and define "good" presentations. Rules like "Always stand to the left of the screen," "Never cross the beam of the projector," and "Remain detached during the presentation."

Those rules are plain stupid! They hamstring you and keep you away from the real stuff—the mystical secret sauce of great presentations: your authentic self.

I once worked with an executive at an insurance company who was a really rotten presenter. He stood stiffly back by the screen and froze every time he stumbled on a word. And he was actually presenting something he really loved—his team's record-beating success! Take this guy off the stage, however, and one-on-one he was a gregarious, funny man. He'd been verbally whipped by so many coaches to follow the rules of presenting that his confidence was blown. He felt trapped in the space up by the screen and miles away from the audience.

I suggested he just be himself—to literally do whatever the heck made him comfortable. So he stood right at the front of the stage where he could see his audience's faces. Sometimes he stepped off the stage. In some parts of the presentation he even gave himself permission to sit down right in the audience! He was miked, so everyone could hear him, and the audience loved how he became one of them rather than a distant expert on stage.

Leaving the stage, stumbling over words, and sitting down would all be considered classic "mistakes." Who cares? What really mattered was that the audience connected with the success of this executive—his team beat all the records. And he suddenly felt connected again to his message, his excitement, and his audience. His voice and body loosened up, he stopped stumbling on words, and his stories became funny again. All this happened because he'd found a way to really be himself in his presentations, and that's what worked.

And here's the thing: if presentations really didn't matter, we'd all just send memos. There are a million ways out there to share information, but no matter how much we digitize, we end up wanting human connection. We pay big money to see recording stars and great thinkers in person because their music and words touch us. And yes, it's really important for people to hear you speak, too. Suppose you're spearheading the effort to build a community park. You can have phone conversations, write letters to the editor, and start a community blog until you're blue in the face. But when the advocates for a new park decide to get together, they want to hear your story. They want to connect with *you*, not a proxy of you.

I'm here to give you the ultimate out—the ultimate freedom. Be human, be you, make mistakes! Don't worry about all the rules you've been taught. People would rather see you, warts and all, if you can communicate with passion. And that's when all the things you want will follow—jobs, funding, support, partners, believers.

So do it! Your way.

It's time for a longitudinal change in how we approach

presentations. It's time to turn what we consider "bad" on its head and reconsider what matters. The reason most people believe they're bad presenters is that they're bound by archaic rules that make them stiff and uncomfortable. This book is about giving yourself permission to be who you are and to present in a way that is authentically yours—mistakes and all. Everyone has something important to say. We all want to change people's minds about issues that really matter to us.

And if being the real you is "bad" according to nasty old rules, then let's change the definition. Just like Michael Jackson, you are now bad in the coolest way. Come on, people, say it with me —"I'm BAD."

We're all ready to break these rules. As a society, we have evolved, even if our presentation primers haven't. We prefer scratchy authenticity to plastic perfection. We are much more likely to trust an online vlogger than a slick scripted commercial. The vlogger's very mistakes, imperfections, and scruffy jeans make her more believable and appealing. And what's more, when she speaks enthusiastically about her opinions, we're drawn in like suntanned kids to a Slip 'n Slide. Now imagine a report given by an impeccably dressed executive who spouts corporate acronyms without cracking a smile. It's like comparing Velveeta to local artisanal cheese. We don't want scary processed-block perfection. We want the real deal—lumps, imperfections, and all.

And there's another reason the authentic stuff is yummier. Artisanal cheese is made by masters who've been at it for decades, whereas Velveeta comes from a factory. We respect mastery—produced by an authentic expert. We realize that they know their stuff and are willing to listen even if they aren't polished. You can be a master, too. You know about something that people would love to hear about. And you can also master being an effective presenter in a way that feels right to you.

> **In eloquent speaking it is the manner that wins, not the words.... You are uniquely yourself— unlike anyone else in this world—and that is what you must project to an audience.**
>
> *—Elbert Hubbard*

Still skeptical? You have every right to be. "If everyone thinks I'm a 'bad' presenter, how do I get to the cool kind of bad?"

I understand. So consider this. I'm fortunate to have worked with more than one thousand people in discovering the best way to be themselves in presentations. Whether they are professional speakers in front of a huge audience, a manager giving a quarterly report via teleconference, or a mom talking to the PTA committee, they can all find power and passion in being authentic. And that often means breaking all the old rules.

You see, I'm an improviser. I've been on the stage since I was five, and improv comedy is the core of my business and philosophy. Improvisation is about freedom, positivity, leapfrogging boundaries, and thinking on your feet. It's about questioning all the rules, throwing out the script, and making it up as you go along. And that core philosophy has allowed me to make a career and life of throwing away all the outdated rules of training and presenting. Shy, skeptical, and gruff people have gone through my company's courses and walked out transformed. Scientists, accountants, attorneys, engineers, editors, introverts, and

extroverts have all figured out that they get to be who they are—
and who they are is *good*.

A leader once told me: "I thought you were going to polish my
team, but what I got was even better. They're authentic. I don't
care anymore that they're not perfect, but I suddenly care about
what they're saying." I don't want you to be a plastic version of
me or anyone else. I do want you to throw out all the rules, get
rid of your fear of mistakes, be excited, and dig into your personal power.

I'm going to be drawing on the powerful tools of improvisation and theater to help you break rules. So let's look at how to
begin the transformation, how to give yourself permission, and
how to stop freezing. Let's look at passion.

**The thing that is really hard, and really
amazing, is giving up being perfect and
beginning the work of becoming yourself.**

—*Anna Quindlen*

BE PASSIONATELY BAD

Passion—what you care about most—is the core of authenticity.
It's the real deal, and you have it. Somewhere under all those nasty
restrictions and buttoned-up rules, there's a rock star inside you.

It doesn't matter whether you love your business, your kids,
your boat, or your basketball team. And passion isn't always about
loving something. Many folks are passionate about changing

something. They work tirelessly to raise money and awareness about disease. They give up their own comfort to provide aid to victims of disaster or poverty. They face their own demons and addictions to show others it's possible to live a better life.

Passion comes in many forms, but there is a common thread. It lights and drives us. It's a special part of our psyche, values, and beliefs. We can talk about our passion for hours, and it's always interesting to us.

And the best part is that in a presentation, *passion overrides technique*. Audiences would much rather watch someone who is passionate about his or her topic, who isn't polished and perfect on stage, than someone who is slick and soulless. And here's wonderful news: audiences want you to do well! They are not out to get you—they really want you to be fabulously bad, and *love* seeing your passionate, quirky self. (More on this when we break Rule #3.)

Passion uses emotion to engage attention. It actually draws in your audience. In her essay, "How to Fascinate," Sally Hogshead explains:

> Think back to a time…when you were leading a presentation and your audience was completely focused on you…. They were lowering the barriers of cynicism and inertia. They stopped merely listening to you, and started connecting with you. This moment—of intense emotional focus—is when you have an opportunity to persuade.[1]

You want to know where presentation power comes from? Passion. In our trainings, my company has participants give an extemporaneous presentation on something they feel passionate about. You would not believe what I've seen. I have been utterly flabbergasted more times than I can count. People who have been boring or stiff will transform completely. I don't even recognize them. It's as though a new person walked into the room—someone I haven't met until now—and I'm blown away by their confidence, clarity, and energy.

I'll never forget one man. I'll call him Sam. He was a new safety manager for an energy provider that distributes electricity, natural gas, and water in the United States. Sam had just been promoted from the field. He'd suddenly gone from digging ditches for power lines to having to provide critical safety presentations to the people who used to dig with him. In his first formal presentation, he couldn't even finish a sentence. He was so nervous and miserable, he tried to bail out three times. We encouraged him, and by clutching a safety booklet and reading it verbatim, he was able to whisper his way through. He kept saying, "I can't do this. I'm terrible. I can't do this."

When we got to the passion exercise, my expectations were low. I expected Sam to speak a few sentences and get off the stage. I could not have been more wrong. He couldn't wait to tell us all about building dune buggies and four-wheelers. He stood up straight, smiled, and joked about his wife having to put up with all the mess in the garage—and oh my. When he related the experience of driving over beaches, the thrill and pleasure he got from it, we were all transported. It was as though we were there in the buggy with him, the radio blasting. Sam even taught at-risk youth how to refurbish vehicles, how to drive and fix them, and how to find a career. When he finished, we all sat stunned for a moment. Even his colleagues couldn't react, they were so surprised. But once we started applauding, we couldn't stop.

Your passion allows you to be... well, *you*. As a matter of fact, most people don't know what they look like when speaking passionately. I'll bet you light up like Rockefeller Center during the holidays when you get going.

When you are connected to who you are, all the stuff that gets in the way is diminished. And by the way, anyone watching you doesn't care as much about technicalities. When Sam was talking about zipping along in his dune buggy, I was busy visualizing the sand, sunset, and speed. I wouldn't have noticed if he had used some incorrect grammar or stuck his hand in his pocket. I just wanted to see more of this interesting, funny guy.

Here's what I'm asking you to do: go deep. What really matters to you? Knowing about your passion is critical to bringing power to your presentations.

This is also the point where some people suddenly feel stuck.

"Well, of course I do well talking about something fun or meaningful. But what do I do when I'm stuck with that boring quarterly report? How can passion possibly apply to that?"

That's the key. Finding out what's important to you, no matter the topic, is one of the trickiest but most effective ways to be really bad in the best way. Even the driest topic can be animated by passion—you just have to identify how you connect to it. I'll talk about that next.

Ring the bells that still can ring.
Forget your perfect offering.
There is a crack in everything.
That's how the light gets in.

—Leonard Cohen, "Anthem"

APPLYING PASSION TO WORK

I worked with an impressive manager at an East Coast Internet and cable service provider. I'll call him Todd. Todd's first presentation was about the company's health and wellness program. Sounds great, but Todd looked like he had the flu while presenting—he was visibly unhappy. He actually said, right before he began, "I'm warning you, this is going to be really boring."

And it *was* boring! He just delivered the outline of the program and a bunch of numbers. Something wasn't clicking. He happened to be a very fit, active guy, naturally excited about health and wellness. It took some digging, but we finally figured out that Todd was disappointed with a major portion of the program. Employees weren't embracing one of the offerings—it was a waste of the company's time and money, which frustrated him intensely.

Todd really liked the walking and smart-diet portions of the program. He felt they were financially efficient, and they were extensively embraced by employees. So I challenged him: could he present his thoughts about slimming down the program to the company's leadership and focus on the parts that really worked? It was like someone had just thrown him a surprise party—he laughed and started working on his new presentation right away. He was passionate about the health and wellness program. Passionate about making it good rather than wasteful.

Now, let's take a reality check here. Presenting your opinion on company programs is not always possible. It can risk your reputation or even your job. We made sure to question Todd closely about the appropriateness of this action. Luckily, he was in a position where he could state opinions freely. And let's not forget, when he was fueled by his passionate belief that the program could really work, he made a powerful presentation. He didn't go in and complain. He went in to convince his audience that he had a more effective, more budget-conscious option so that they would reorganize the program. He used his passion to create and present options that were well received. What started out as a boring corporate chore became an opportunity to make a difference.

Try applying this to your own work. I'm sure you've been stuck with presenting a quarterly report or a department update that made *you* want to fall asleep, let alone your audience. Where's the passion in that? It's there, but some rigor is needed to find it. Any information you present has some connection to you. Try taking the time to ask why it matters:

> › How does this apply to me?

> › If I could change anything in this situation, what would it be? Can I talk about that?

> › If this is the most important thing I'm doing today, how can I find the powerful part of it?

> › What piece of this do I really care about?

> › If I don't care, why is that? What could change to make me care?

Those questions allow you to pause in the midst of your busy life and consider what matters to you. Examining motivations, opinions, and thoughts on any topic allows anyone to present in a more meaningful way. When working with presenters, I'm surprised how often they've forgotten to ask themselves why they are doing what they are doing. And time spent digging a little deeper is well spent—it enables your ability to connect to passion and meaning, no matter what the topic.

Channel your passion—find surprising places where it might apply. I'll be sharing more stories of people who took boring updates, applied their passion, and came out fabulously bad.

But before we move on, let me make an important point.

Does this mean that if you're passionate, nothing else in presentations matters? No. Being both passionate *and* effective in your presentations is the magic combination. It means that passion can transform you, elevate you, connect you with your audience. The questions to ask are "How can I be myself and bring my passion out?" "How can I show it without being so crazy or emotional that I sink my own ship?"

Rethink your approach to speaking. Instead of focusing your preparation and presentations on following rules, start centering them on *you*. What matters? What do you want to accomplish? How can you have the most fun?

And whatever you do, break any rules that don't work for you!

For a short video on Passion,
visit www.ImprovEdge.com/videos

ONE

THE BADDEST WAY TO PREPARE

Start Breaking the Rules Before You Even Hit the Stage

There's just too much going on in presentations: information to remember, slides crammed with data, your pulse racing, and all those rotten rules to follow. Focus, people, focus! You need to peel away the excess stuff that gets in the way of efficient, authentic presenting.

Let's put on our geek hats and consider why this matters. Neuroscience is uncovering more and more information about the importance of focus. David Rock and Jeffrey Schwartz have done insanely cool research into how our brains connect to our leadership abilities and to our everyday human behavior. As we dump behaviors that stand in our way (i.e., break old rules) and replace them with new ways to focus our thoughts and energy, we are actually rewiring our brains. Being ourselves becomes easier and easier if we focus on it.

> Over time, paying enough attention to any specific brain connection keeps the relevant circuitry open and dynamically alive. These circuits can then eventually become not just chemical links but stable, physical changes in the brain's structure... the brain changes as a function of where an individual puts his or her attention. The power is in the focus.[1]

So instead of focusing on what you're doing wrong (which the rules of presenting just *love* to do), focus on your strengths and being yourself. Get this: if you focus on new behaviors, you can change your brain to embrace patterns that make you a better, more authentic speaker. Rock and Schwartz call it "attention density," and it applies to many areas of human behavior, as well as mood and learning skills. Put simply, if you start presenting in new ways, your brain will open up circuits to support your confidence and capabilities. If that doesn't make you feel like you have a bionic brain, I don't know what will.

In Appreciative Inquiry, we find that the things which you focus upon, grow.
—David Cooperrider and Diana Whitney

Passion and focus may seem like surprising ideas with which to begin talking about presentations. Most discussions start with the rules. But trust me: it's all part of the business of getting down to business. If you can let your passion out of the stable to run free, you can certainly try a few new techniques to replace the old rules.

There's impact and influence in knowing just what you want to share and doing it at just the right time. And that means you can use techniques that feel right for you. Whenever a technique gets in the way of you being authentic, it's time to break the rules.

So let's do it. Let's break fourteen of those archaic rules and instead present in a way that feels good, fun, and really *bad*.

#1: Your purpose is to give a good presentation

"Good" is to a presentation like "fine" is to a compliment. Your purpose is to make something happen!

Rule to Break #1 is mired in technicality. There you stand, waiting for your chance to speak to the committee, and all you're worried about is "giving a good presentation." What does that mean? It means you're obsessed with all the wrong things: your slides show every number in existence, you say everything in order, you stand up straight behind the podium, you never cross the beam of the projector, and you don't pass out. You're drowning in worry because the only thing rolling around in your head is, "Give a good presentation. Give a good presentation. Don't mess up, and give a good presentation!"

It's time to have a heart-to-heart with yourself about why you're standing there. What purpose does this presentation serve? Having a searingly clear purpose will filter out all the silt from your presentation. Think of purpose as the destination—the outcome of your presentation. What do you want to have happen? What great change will come from you taking the time to talk to these people? Consider Todd from the Internet and cable company. The purpose of his new presentation was to convince his company's leadership to cut out the wasteful portion of the health and wellness program and keep the good parts. He wanted to make something happen.

Your purpose is the "so what" for your audience and your driving goal. Here are some examples:

> You want to convince the committee to *increase your budget by 10 percent next year.*

> You want to entertain the youth club so that they *enter the state go-cart competition.*

> You want to inspire college students to *vote for the first time.*

> You want to anger your community council so that they *enact laws to protect the environment.*

> You want to motivate a client to dump its old vendor and *buy your products instead.*

Purpose has to be tied to an outcome—what do you want your audience to do as a result of your work? You make something happen because your passionate presentation had a purpose.

Purpose is critical because it colors all your decisions about the presentation. With a purpose, you can suddenly make clear decisions about content and flow. If you really want kids to enter the state go-cart competition, don't tell them about seven different kinds of toys they could build and just hope that they decide to make go-carts. You focus on go-carts and tell stories about other kids who have won!

If you want your budget to be increased by 10 percent, don't review all department budgets, the corporate marketing plan, and the company picnic. Talk about your success and map out how you would use the additional funds to benefit your company. Suddenly, slides, comments, and quotations that don't support your purpose are easily trashed.

One of the most obvious signs of a purposeless presentation is a tsunami of information. When you're drowning your audience in data, it's because you're not sure where you're going. You just hope that all the information will move the audience in the right direction.

I worked with the chief strategy officer of a national insurer and her direct team—a small group of about eight people who were incredibly intelligent, data-driven, and numbers-oriented. The team was also in a very delicate position. They needed to influence decisions but didn't necessarily have the power to tell people what to do, and that included the CEO!

The team's presentations made my brain feel like it was on novocaine. Numbers, numbers, everywhere, and not a purpose in sight. One participant was trying to influence the company's leaders to invest in car-safety technology. But you'd never know that. He saw his role as that of the informer. He threw tons of data at the audience and hoped enough stuck to move them in his direction. We in the audience were busy reading slides covered with data. Whenever we did have a chance to listen, he overwhelmed us with his racer-fast delivery of acronyms and scientific projections. I eventually removed the fire hose from my mouth and asked him, "What are you trying to accomplish?"

Once he focused and agreed to hone in on one purpose, everything changed. He clearly stated his purpose, used only the data that directly supported investment in car-safety technology, and talked about the benefits of that one idea. He cut out confusing information and moved toward a single outcome. That, in turn, allowed him to communicate a powerful, simple message. Most importantly, he influenced listeners without seeming to do so.

It was like in *The Wizard of Oz*, when the black-and-white screen gives way to Technicolor.

This concept also applies to one-on-one meetings or conversations around a table. We've all been in way too many purposeless meetings and conversations. Think about how much more productive, clear, and short those meetings would be if they had a purpose. For example, "We're going to discuss only digital marketing and decide on the first step today." Whenever someone starts to careen into on-site advertising, they're wrangled back to the purpose. "Let's decide where to go on vacation with the current budget." Whenever topics such as what you'd do with more money or what to pack comes up—screech! Put on the brakes and bring it all back.

So, keep it simple. It's best to walk in with one strong purpose, accomplish that, and move on to another purpose at another time. I've seen presenters try to accomplish two, three, or four purposes at once, and you can guess what happens. Nothing. The audience walks out not knowing what to do.

And every now and then, your purpose can be very selfish and a little secret—no one else has to know what it is. There's nothing wrong with choosing a purpose such as impressing the boss so that she gives you a promotion or making your children laugh so that they think cleaning up is fun and you can do less of it. All your audience will know is that you gave a very compelling presentation and they're coming around quickly to your suggestions.

Purpose is the ace in the hole. It gives you focus, drive, and clarity.

For a short video on Purpose, visit
www.ImprovEdge.com/videos

#2: Give informational presentations

That's about as exciting as watching grass grow. Take action!

You've got a destination—your purpose. Now, how are you going to get there? You need a vehicle, and that's your action. Action is the way you go about accomplishing your purpose. In other words, how you get there. Purpose = What. Action = How.

Action is probably the single most critical reason that presentations even occur. Remember when I said that if you're just going to hand over a bunch of data, why not send out an email or a memo? You're there in person for a reason, because your passion, purpose, and energy are going to affect people. Action is how you will make them feel. It is an emotional connection to the audience that moves them—and drives your purpose. By choosing an action, you're going to make people feel something, consider new ideas, maybe even get mad. You will be:

> motivating

> convincing

> entertaining

> angering

> invigorating

> teaching

> inspiring

Your action is the driving force that gives power to your presentation. Remember my examples of a purpose in the previous chapter? Let's look at them again, now with the action words in italic:

> You want to *convince* the committee to increase your budget by 10 percent next year.

> You want to *entertain* the youth club so that they enter the state go-cart competition.

> You want to *inspire* college students to vote for the first time.

> You want to *anger* your community council so that they enact laws to protect the environment.

> You want to *motivate* a client to dump its old vendor and buy your products instead.

Much like purpose, action helps you—the presenter—to focus. You *know* what you want to make happen, so you focus your delivery. You're there to entertain the youth club. So don't present boring information about the number of boards the kids need, the width of the boards, and the length of the nails. Talk about the wind in their hair as their go-carts race along at top speed. Talk about meeting other kids at the state competition and the cool prizes. Tell funny stories about your first awful, lopsided go-cart and how proud you were when you learned to do it right.

Do you think it's an accident that every college-student organization has pizza at its meetings? Students are always hungry—you feed them, and they see you as a friend. Then you whip up their natural desire to be part of something exciting. You use stories about how one vote can win an election, making their voice heard, being part of real change. All those steps lead to inspiring them to vote for the first time. And better yet, tell them you'll drive them to the polls, and the deal is done.

Or if you're there to motivate your client to switch to your products, be sure they're aware of your competitor's falling stock price and the fact that the other guys source their devices from a foreign country. Give your client compelling reasons why you're a better bet so that they're motivated to go through the difficult process of dropping a vendor and starting with a new one.

Purpose and action are rooted in the theater. Great actors, improvisers, and speakers drive their work with action and purpose. When you see a great performance on the screen, one that moves you, makes you laugh or cry, it's because an actor has chosen a purpose and an action for his character. Hamlet's single purpose was to find out who killed his father, the king. His actions were to threaten, confuse, and outsmart the other characters until he found the murderer.

I had a wonderful early career in improv, stage, and film. I eventually left that life and went to work in technology—network engineering—in New York City. What a switch! Even though I was working hard and cramming at night, I often had no idea what the heck I was talking about. So I had a purpose and an action for every meeting and presentation. I may still have been learning the fine points, but I absolutely understood the big picture of what I was after: a signed contract, a raise, or a partnership program. I thought about the people I was trying to influence, then I used data to convince them. Or funny stories to entertain them. Or falling stock prices to scare the doo-doo out of them.

But there's one very sticky issue with action. This is the

baddest piece of my bad advice. Remove "inform" from your list of acceptable actions. Notice it's not on the list at the start? If you use it, cross it out permanently. Inform is a cop-out. It is the default action for 95 percent of presentations, and it's one of the weakest choices you can make. Think about it—most presentations are approached with an attitude like, "I'll give them all the information, and then I've done my job. If they do nothing, it's not my fault. I'm just there to inform." Gee thanks, milquetoast.

In the worst case, the action of informing removes responsibility from the presenter for having a greater purpose for being there. It drains energy and diffuses focus. And that's when extraneous data and unrelated points start to find their way in. Computers, machines, and spreadsheets inform. Humans interpret and find deeper meaning in numbers and information.

I challenge you to always choose a more powerful option than inform. Even a standard update can teach, motivate, or convince an audience.

I have a real-life example from my work with a regional sports media provider. One woman in my group, Susan, belligerently insisted that it was impossible for her quarterly updates to do anything other than inform. Updates are just that—information. So why should she care about doing anything else but laying out the info as quickly as possible and being done with it?

I asked her about the audience: she gave her presentation to an assistant to the CEO, and that assistant would then brief the CEO. So I nudged her. What might be the worst outcome of that process? She admitted that the assistant could develop all sorts of unbecoming perceptions. For example, she might presume that Susan wasn't very committed, that the department was barely meeting its goals for the year, or that their ideas or attitude didn't align with the company's goals—which would then result in an unfavorable report to the CEO. A report like that could mean budget cuts, uncomplimentary reviews, or even firings. It turned out that this assistant had a great deal more influence than Susan had really considered.

What about the best-case scenario? Susan shared that the best outcome would be for the assistant to return surprised and excited about the department's great work and voice her approval to the CEO. That could result in more funding for the department, positive performance reviews, and promotions. By focusing on the potential impact of this "standard" presentation, Susan realized how much influence she could have.

Susan changed her entire approach. For the next quarterly update, she and her team agreed on a purpose: having such good reviews from the assistant that they would be awarded a budget increase at the end of the year. Their action was to inspire her to comment positively to the CEO and support their recommendations for more funds. With that focus, the team's members gave the best update they had ever made. They integrated success stories, creatively shared their ideas, and used bright posters in a sunny room rather than PowerPoint slides in a dark room. For the first time, the assistant asked questions, laughed, and commented on the information. With each successive update, Susan and her team drove home their purpose in more and more creative ways to engage and inspire the assistant. And—you guessed it. At the end of the year, Susan and her team got a budget increase for the next year.

Susan connected to the information in a personal way. That filled her with the passion to have a clear purpose and action. By combining those elements, she and her team enjoyed an incredible outcome.

Action is the vehicle that gets you to your destination, the purpose. Choose a strong action, and you'll add fuel to your next presentation!

**For a short video on Action,
visit www.ImprovEdge.com/videos**

#3: Practice in front of a mirror

Mirrors are just a one-person show. Practice often, out loud, and on your feet!

Practicing in front of a mirror sounds like great advice. We don't know what we look like, and it's not always possible to videotape our practice, so why not? This rule is one of those that everybody knows is "right."

> To give yourself the best possible chance of playing to your potential, you must prepare for every eventuality. That means practice.
>
> —*Seve Ballesteros*

I've heard or read this tip countless times, and here's what happens when you practice in front of a mirror: You get used to performing for an "audience" that's about twelve inches away. You become obsessed with how you hold your face, the arc of your arm, and that part of your body you don't like. You think about yourself and how you look. You worry about tics you didn't notice before, or conversely, you really enjoy smiling back at that good-looking person in the mirror. In short, you practice watching yourself.

You're supposed to be practicing watching the audience! You won't be watching yourself when you present, but your body, voice, and energy will all be used to a mirror, which gives no feedback, reaction, or energy and makes you focus on yourself. Nothing will make you self-conscious and inwardly focused more quickly than practicing in front of a mirror.

There's a Greek legend about a hunter named Narcissus, who was renowned for his beauty. He was quite proud, so Nemesis decided to act. Nemesis was the goddess of retribution against those who succumbed to hubris, or overarching pride. She lured Narcissus to a pool where he saw his reflection. He fell in love with his own beauty and eventually wasted away and died, staring at his own reflection. Psychology has an illness named for the hunter—narcissism.

Merriam-Webster's dictionary defines narcissism as "egoism, egocentrism," and synonyms include self-absorption and self-centeredness. Of course, most people aren't remotely narcissists, but a mirror can make anyone worry too much about themselves. Too much self-reflection removes your focus from the audience. You just keep coming back to the reflection, rather than to reality. If we're centered on ourselves, instead of on our audiences, we'll kill a good presentation.

To feel the difference between a mirror and an open room, put your hand up in front of your face as though it's a mirror. Notice how it's several inches away, blocks your view of anything else, and makes the area around you feel small. When you practice in that "space," you keep your energy close and don't project your voice. Now stand at the front of an open room and look around. You can see all the way to the back wall. You realize that your energy and voice need to project to the front, sides, and rear of the room. You begin to notice details about the room and how you feel standing at the front.

This is the best way to practice presentations—in an open

room, your hotel room, or a conference room. Get used to how your body feels and your voice sounds. Stumble through, mess up—so what. It's practice. And do it with an audience if you can swing it. Your best friend, spouse, or colleague will give you better feedback than any mirror ever will. You'll feel what it's like to have another person react to you, and you'll understand how energy and eye contact affect them.

Sure, practicing in front of a mirror, maybe once, might help you become aware of how you look. That's not an awful thing, but you've got to step away and feel the excitement and fear of facing a room. You may not look perfect, and that's just fine.

The whole world's a stage and most of us are desperately unrehearsed.

—Seán O'Casey

Real, on-your-feet preparation—there's no substitute. I had a man come up to me after a workshop laughing ruefully. "I was hoping your workshop would give me an out. I was looking for the magic pill; how I can be fabulous without practice. You just verified that there are no shortcuts."

Sorry, kids. Even when you're breaking all the rules, you've got to practice your badness! And I promise it's worth it. There's a staggering trend I've been tracking. My study isn't scientific, and I've not formally recorded the numbers, but at workshop after workshop, the people in the most senior positions are always the most prepared. They set aside time to organize, practice speeches out loud, or simply work through the purpose for their next meeting. This makes it pretty obvious how they got to that top job, doesn't it? These people tell me stories about their solid preparation habits even when they weren't at a senior level. People who are less experienced or lower in the org chart rush around making sure we know how busy they are—and wing it, wing it, wing it. Yep, the people who most need to prepare are the least likely to do so.

I mean, come on. Do you really think Olympic athletes wing it?

Author Malcolm Gladwell studied people at the top of their fields. He found that it wasn't innate talent or intelligence that sent people to the top of their professions. It was practice and experience. He contends that it takes about ten thousand hours of real-time practice to catapult someone to the highest level of capabilities—whether as a computer programmer, concert pianist, athlete, or member of a rock 'n' roll band. The people who put in the time, work, and practice are the ones who excel. The Beatles, for example, played marathon eight-hour sets at strip clubs in advance of their celebrity. They had performed more than twelve hundred times before their first burst of fame in 1964.

That magic number—ten thousand hours—continues to pop up as the differentiator between people who work hard and do well, and those who work really, really hard and do incredibly well.[2] Or in our case, are super bad.

So, what about natural talent? Believe it or not, there's more danger here for those who are naturally comfortable presenters, and less for those who are nervous and uncertain. People who know they need practice might at least feel guilty when they don't prepare. But I have a special warning for those who often receive praise and feel they can pull off a pretty good presentation without preparation. Your advantage is that you have tricks and natural grace that allow you to wing it. Your disadvantage is that you believe that's all you need. And the more you get used to winging it, the less time you'll devote to improvement. That's a mistake. Tony Schwartz, who has aggregated studies on this topic, says this:

> If you're not actively working to get better at what you do, there's a good chance you're getting worse, no matter what the quality of your initial training—in some cases, diminished performance is simply the result of a failure to keep up with the advances in a given field. But it's also because most of us tend to become fixed in our habits and practices, even when they're suboptimal.[3]

I once had a member of my ensemble who was magnetic and smart but never prepared until the day of an event. Under pressure, it was clear that he hadn't looked up any new material and had not prepared very much. He could always come off as good and charming, but pretty soon I knew his entire bag of tricks and was onto his style. He lacked depth. I knew I'd never be able to send him to a client more than twice—they too would grow weary of his same old delivery. Buh-bye.

What we're talking about here is a plateau. When you reach a certain level of competence, your body and mind realize that it's good enough to get by on. And let's be honest—society rewards a certain level of competence and often doesn't expect more. The author Joshua Foer calls this concept the "OK Plateau." You're okay at something, you're competent, but despite months, even years, of practice, you do not improve. Foer's examples include typing—once we are able to type at a certain acceptable speed, we might remain at that speed for the rest of our lives despite hours of time spent typing.[4] We can discover why with a deeper look at practice.

It's not necessarily the hours and hours you spend typing that allow you to improve. Truly improving requires conscious effort: trying more difficult techniques, pushing to increase your speed, and being willing to fail. The researchers K. Anders Ericsson, Ralf Krampe, and Clemens Tesch-Romer studied this phenomenon and called it "deliberate practice." Practice and experience are absolutely necessary to becoming a better typist, a better athlete, a better presenter. The more you do, the more situations and surprises you encounter, the better you become. However, only those who continually stretch, experiment, and fail will move toward expertise.[5]

The Beatles were great by 1964 because of the inordinate amount of performing hours they had put in. But the second key here is that they had to keep getting better and playing new material. They had to cover hundreds of songs by dozens of bands and keep writing original songs. Otherwise, audiences would become bored with their set, and the club owners wouldn't hire them anymore. In the process of rehearsing, performing, and learning more complicated music, you can bet that The Beatles failed more times than they would ever admit. Every failure prodded them toward true expertise.[6]

If I don't practice the way I should, then I won't play the way that I know I can.

—Ivan Lendl

Most people don't know that improvisers are the most over-rehearsed people in the performance industry. Surprised? You may think improvisers are just quick on their feet and throw it all together. But the truth is that improv troupes rehearse more

than twice as much as casts for Shakespeare plays. They have to—
there's no script, and no two performances are alike. Improv is an
art form that happens in the moment without a script, props, or
a plan, so improvisers spend exorbitant amounts of time practicing every possible scenario on stage. That's why, when you see a
great improv show, it looks effortless. The key is that during practice, the troupe is always trying to surprise each other—coming
up with the weirdest, most difficult audience suggestions imag-
inable. (And believe me, even the broadest imagination sometimes falls short of what an audience member will shout out.)

You know where I'm going with this. You've got to practice.
Out loud, often, and on your feet. If you're one of the lucky people who has natural ability, understand that you're the most
likely to become stagnant. If you're terrified, nervous, and inex-
perienced, you have nowhere to go but up. Practice will make an
astonishing difference in your ability to be effective, influential,
and wow your audience. Most of the problems I first see when
people present can usually be ironed out with two or three run-
throughs. Do any of these sound familiar?

> **Running long or out of time**—Reading through your
  speech silently or whispering it to yourself will never
  approximate the true amount of time it will take to say it
  out loud and on your feet. And the more you practice, the
  more you will become aware of time. We often ask people
  to prepare a three-minute presentation, and they have no
  idea that their time is up when they've barely completed
  their intro. As you practice, your body will actually be able
  to feel how much time has passed because you'll become
  accustomed to how long it takes to get through certain
  amounts of material.

> **Stumbling over your words**—If you don't say them out loud, you won't realize that the brilliant phrases you've written or imagined are impossible to say. Lyricists know that even if they believe their words will fit a song perfectly, they never really know until someone tries to sing it.

> **Going up or going blank**—"Going up" is a theater term for when an actor forgets a major part of the script and skips ahead. That's always a scramble because then the other actors have to figure out a way to justify what's happening! "Going blank" is, of course, entirely forgetting what you're supposed to say. One of the most common reasons for going blank is that you've never given your body, voice, and mind the experience of standing in front of an open room, sea of faces, or group of chairs. You get messed up by the acoustics of the room, the distraction of the people in it, or simply the sensation of trying to hold yourself in a standing position.

Improvisation works only after an enormous amount of thought and practice.

—*Rafael Viñoly*

So do it! Start practicing and get used to stumble-throughs. People often want to bail out when their first run-through is rough. But that's the point. It should be ragged, difficult, and full of mistakes. Then you figure out what to change. The next time is a little better, and the next even better. Why would you want to submit your audience, and that critical speech, to your first unpleasant dry run? In her book *Bird by Bird*, Anne Lamott makes a wonderful point about writing that applies here. She notes that all good writers write terrible first drafts.[7] So, if a rotten first draft, or an awful first run-through, is part of the process, why not embrace it?

Many of us deal with a lot of fear when we're faced with presenting to a crowd. That's natural. Practice will help manage that fear. I'm not going to promise that it will ever go away completely, but it's a part of you, and the more you get back on that horse, the better rider you'll become.

Practice isn't the thing you do once you're good. It's the thing you do that makes you good.

—*Malcolm Gladwell*

My favorite piece of bad advice is that you present in every low-risk venue you can scare up. It's better to experiment in a place where you don't have so much at stake. Groups everywhere would love to hear you speak: your local youth club on baking a holiday cake, your place of worship on managing finances, your book club on meeting an author. There are tons of places where you can try out a new hook or practice moving around the stage. That way, you'll have places to fail, get up, try again, and figure out what works for you. Then when it is time to give a critical speech to a committee at work, you'll be confident and ready.

And heck yeah, I know you're busy! And I know you really want to skip this part because you only present once per quarter. But if you start baking practice into your schedule, even a little bit, you'll be a badder you. Book time on your calendar, leave your home or office, or promise your friends cookies if they'll watch you for thirty minutes. Whatever it takes. When the presentation is down pat, you can handle all the little unexpected things that might come up and just be yourself—rather than going blank because you didn't practice. This is about *doing*.

For a short video on Practice,
visit www.ImprovEdge.com/videos

#4: Picture the audience in their underwear

Stupid visuals distance you. Connect with your audience. Who really wants to visualize Bob from accounting in his underwear?

How many sitcoms have spoofed this rule? The goofy main character has to speak to an audience, or the high schooler has to address her classmates. So some wise mentor suggests, in order to control the student's nerves, that she should picture the audience in their underwear. The theory is that this visualization lowers the intimidation factor of the scary audience, tickles the presenter, and makes her relax.

Seriously?

I've tried it, and I've even had test subjects try it. It's distracting, makes you go blank, and leaches energy away from your passion and funnels it to a stupid technique. And there's always someone in the first row whom I really *don't* want to visualize in underwear. Ick.

The *Presentation Rulebook* is just full of dumb tips like this one. Sure, you might be scared of the audience, but let them remain fully clothed in your mind for a while. You are there for your audience, so respect them. Visuals that make you giggly or embarrassed separate you from the audience. And connecting to your audience, in a way that allows you to be yourself, is a key step to winning them over.

And here's a really big deal secret: the audience *wants* you to do well. Audiences are not by nature mean and intimidating. No one shows up hoping to see a presentation tank: "Gee, I hope this guy is really boring and bad. What a great use of my time."

What's more, audience members naturally empathize. If you're visibly nervous, if your technology blows up, or if you can't answer a tough question, the people around you will wish they could help. Audiences are your friends, and they're just dying for you to be brilliant. They're actually pulling for you. Think of them as a quiet cheering section next time you stand up.

The cheering section idea extends to friends and strangers. It's counterintuitive, but you will always be more nervous presenting to ten friends than to one hundred strangers. You'd think that a group of friends would put you at ease, but a familiar audience can actually make you as comfortable as a snowman in a tanning bed. You expect more of yourself in front of friends. Friends know us well, and we figure they'll be harsh critics who notice every weakness. Don't stress out; the same empathy applies here. Your colleagues want you to do well just as much as strangers do. They would love to be pleasantly surprised or maybe even blown away by how awesomely bad you are.

AUDIENCE: THE REASON YOU'RE THERE

Okay, purpose and action are critical, but would you even be in the room if it weren't for the audience? We present because people want or need to hear us talk. If you can figure out who the heck they are and what they want, you can rock your purpose and action:

> › Who?—Youngsters, seniors, executives, circus clowns?

› Why?—Forced to attend by a boss, excited to learn, a potential stalker?

› What do they want?—Action steps, new ideas, your phone number?

› When?—2 p.m. after-lunch slump, after-cocktail-hour tipsy, or when everyone's been stuck in a place for two hours and really needs the bathroom?

› How to reach them?—Funny stories because it's a group of high school kids, smart research because it's a group of analysts, or touching stories because it's a charity lunch.

Understanding the audience members' expectations, their frame of mind, and their physical state can only help you be deliciously bad. As a matter of fact, your choice of purpose and action should be directly driven by the audience.

I just watched a college administrator present to a group of third graders who were receiving honors for their performance on a standardized test. It was painful. She wrote the speech to encourage them to continue to excel academically, but she completely forgot she was talking to third-grade kids. She stood behind a podium and read from a piece of paper strung with long words and sentences about "accessing their online toolbox to better challenge and ascertain their particular strengths in order to reach academic goals that would lead to a more rigorous high school career leading to meaningful college choices." Can't you just see the squirmy ocean of kid despair in that auditorium? *I* wanted to cry for *my* mommy.

And here's the disconnect: I saw her interact one-on-one with the kids beforehand. She was a completely different person. She was friendly, got down on her knees so that she could speak with them eye to eye, and made them giggle. Unfortunately, she had also subscribed to *College Administrators Are Crushingly Boring Presenters* magazine.

What could she have done differently? If you want to encourage young brainiacs to continue to excel, put yourself in their shoes. Common issues for gifted kids include feeling alone, bored, or misunderstood. She might have celebrated what a full auditorium it was and told them that they were surrounded by other smart kids who could be their friends. She might have sat on the lip of the stage so that she could be closer to their level and show a more relaxed, accessible side of herself, rather than appear as a disembodied head over the podium. And if you want to challenge a gifted kid, ask for their ideas. She could have let them come up with ideas about what activities they could do to keep getting smarter. I bet every little hand would have shot up.

Instant connection and credibility. That's what you get if an audience sees that you've thought about and understand them. They'll trust you—and every bridge you build to your audience also gets your mind off yourself. And the sweat trickling down your back. Stay focused on the audience, and your nervousness will lessen. (More about this later when we break Rule #13.)

So what's one of the worst outcomes of not taking your audience into account? Offending them. And then being shown up. I went to a women's networking event once to see a local speaker. Apparently, he was a sales whiz and was going to talk about sales techniques for entrepreneurs and salespeople. He decided to open with an example of a bad sales experience he had had. So he slammed a local retail department store. His story went like this: "I waited in that bargain basement tapping my foot, while the gray-haired old lady behind the counter finished her Harlequin romance and finally decided to ring me up." Who was in his audience? The sales manager and floor team from that very store. One glance at the attendee list at the registration table would have cleared that up. Not to mention that he literally sneered when he told the story. Do you think *any* woman appreciates a man referring to "gray-haired old ladies" and "Harlequin romances" like they're ubiquitous, unavoidable attributes of the female gender? He lost us at "hello."

When he finished his speech and called for questions, the sales manager asked if she could come up and use the mike. He had no idea who she was until she got close enough for her name tag to come into focus. She made a gracious comment about even great people having challenging days, apologized that his sales experience wasn't excellent, and offered him a hefty discount on his next purchase. She then reminded us all that her store strove for excellent customer service. She was so crisp, and so terribly bad in her delivery, that he could only stare, sputter, and eventually mumble a "thank you."

I'm guilty of forgetting my audience, too. I messed this up early in my career. I once conducted a workshop that was peppered with personal stories and theater examples. I had done zippo on my upfront audience prep and considered my stories fascinating. During a break, the organizer gave me a takedown like a WWF champion. "This is a group of high-performing accountants. We do not care about your career or your personal examples." Ouuuuuuuch. I completely deserved it. Their culture and expectations were very specific, and if I had done even a little web research and conducted a few phone calls, I would have known that. One personal story, in the right place, might have been fine. But without showing that I understood their industry,

I tanked my credibility. I changed my approach pronto. I have always been so grateful for this organizer's no-nonsense feedback. It was a gift.

Let me give you another excellent example. Among the participants in the workshops with the energy producer I work with was Ed. At the beginning of the day, Ed gave a standard presentation on company financials. He was the only corporate finance guy in a room full of frontline workers. And I'm not kidding when I tell you he was the only person with a white collar. Everyone's eyes glazed over after about thirty seconds. They just couldn't connect to the presentation. Ed knew it, we all knew it.

Participants always have to redo their presentations to incorporate their learning. What I didn't expect was how this man would transform his delivery based on the audience. He rewired his whole approach. He told stories about how the performance of the frontline workers directly affected the company's profits. Then he showed pictures and talked about what happened when profit was good: the company bought better equipment, offered better employee benefits, and added jobs. Let me tell you, the audience was sitting up in their seats and leaning forward. No one had ever made them feel so clearly connected to the company's finances. It bordered on genius. Ed made a roomful of friends and believers that day.

Now, speaking selfishly, audience attention can also set you apart. I held a conference call with a committee that organized events for their company's leadership. After I asked all my questions about the audience and what the committee wanted, there was a weird silence. I thought my phone had dropped the call. Then the chair said, "You're the only speaker who's ever asked about us. The others just showed up with their canned stuff. You can do two of our next meetings." Whew. What an improvement from my earlier experience.

You raise the bar when you focus on your audience.

READING THE AUDIENCE

Okay, we've kept the audience clothed and done our darnedest to understand them. Now we've got to read their reactions to our speech. People freak out about this one. "I don't know how to read an audience!" Yes, you do. If you're standing in front of a crowd, if you're being yourself and talking about something that matters to you, you'll be able to look around and figure out if you're connecting with them. If the audience is making eye contact with you, nodding a bit, leaning forward, those are good indications that they're listening.

It's not the reading that scares people. It's the responding. Don't confuse reading an audience with responding to it. Almost any human with a pulse knows if they're tanking. Your audience will be squirmy and look away, and people's body language will slump and lose energy. The question is can you change in midstream? Are you willing to step outside your plan to reengage them? That's what reading an audience is about. Changing to serve their needs, not yours.

Imagine that you're standing in front of an audience and notice they're fidgeting. How many of us begin to think "Oh, they must not like me, I must have said something wrong"? You start to shut down, turn your focus inward, and begin to cater to your own needs. You might cut the presentation short or skip a few stories because you think the audience isn't interested. It makes you want to run rather than lean in. Instead, this is when you need to shift your behavior to reconnect with the audience. You could ask for a quick survey of hands: "How many of you have heard about this research before?" Or you might solicit contributions from the audience: "Now that we've covered the technique, could someone from accounting share an example of this method?" Maybe you could let them make a decision as a group: "I have two more models to cover and a case study. Which do you want to hear first?"

You're not there to impress your audience with how remarkable you are; you're there to communicate with them. Concentrate on the positive. Become more "audience involved" and less "me involved." Self-consciousness results from too much attention to yourself, which puts others—your audience—in the background and you at the front.

This is called consciousness vs. self-consciousness. Actors learn early on to focus on their scene partner ("What are they feeling? What are they saying?") in order to be authentic and in the moment. The second an actor retreats into his mind ("How do I look in my costume? I'm going to really play this emotion big to impress that agent in the front row"), he retreats from the scene, which in turn, distances the audience. When you become self-conscious, you lose confidence. But when you focus outside yourself, you reduce the distractions of inner voices and are less self-conscious. You can remain present and powerful. Cool side effects of concentrating on the audience include less nervousness and more fun.

Let's give our audiences a break, too. There are always a kajillion different things that could be affecting your audience on any given day. One of my ensemble members, Zoe, tells a great story about reacting too personally. She was facilitating a workshop and noticed one man in the back who never laughed, seemed bored, and didn't contribute. Zoe became more and more worried about her delivery. She took the man's yawning and glances at his watch and phone personally and began to blame herself mentally for what appeared to be his lack of engagement. She had destructive thoughts like "I must not be engaging enough. He probably knows all this material and is bored. This process isn't working and he doesn't like me!"

During a small-group exercise, she approached him. "I noticed you're kind of quiet. Is everything okay—can I change something to help you engage?" The young man looked surprised and then a bit embarrassed. "Don't change a thing! This is great! I'm sorry, I have a newborn baby at home, and I haven't had a good night's sleep in a couple of weeks." That explanation allowed Zoe to relax, and the young man felt he was understood. He could stay as focused as possible, but he felt no pressure to participate on an intense level. Zoe tells this story as an example of how we can internalize the behavior or body language of an audience member that we don't understand. We personalize someone's behavior rather than becoming curious about it—without realizing that people are influenced by plenty of factors out of our control. The upshot is that she correctly read his body language—he was tired and a bit disengaged. But that didn't mean she was at fault. Zoe tells this story because the situation taught her that while self-awareness is useful, self-consciousness gets in the way of effective presenting. If every indicator you see makes you become reflective to the point of self-consciousness, you're worrying too much. Instead, be curious and open to indicators about the impact you're having as a presenter, and learn with every experience. That's self-awareness. It is a subtle but powerful difference.

You can never assume you know what someone may be thinking. Different people process information and react very differently. A good base standard for engagement is eye contact. A completely quiet audience is fine, as long as they are making eye contact every now and then. They may not be looking at you all the time, as some people need to look down or away to listen fully. Nods and movements that show engagement are also good indicators. These mean people are listening, considering, and staying engaged. You also have auditory cues: laughter, gasps, scoffs of disbelief, or uh-huhs of agreement let you know you're affecting the audience.

Sometimes reading your audience also involves being a bit of a chameleon. Before jumping into a presentation, it's great if you can move around the room, watch your audience, or even speak with some of them in advance. That way you can tweak your energy or your delivery to appeal to the audience. No doubt you've heard of the Golden Rule: "Treat others as you would like to be treated." That's okay until you come up against someone who doesn't have your preferences. A better standard is the Platinum Rule: "Treat others the way that *they* would like to be treated." This means communicating in a way that best appeals to the other person, not to you. (I *do* get the irony of referencing a rule in a book about breaking them.)

A perfect example is a meeting with a boss. I've talked to so many people who don't understand why they're not building a good relationship with their boss. It's usually because of style—you may be very extroverted and want to chat a lot about family to connect with others. Your boss, on the other hand, may be a very data-driven, get-to-the-point thinker. She's waiting for you to shut up and get to the numbers, but you keep chatting in the hope that she'll relax and open up. Yikes! This is a clear difference in personality. Building a good relationship in this instance probably has a lot to do with observing and listening. What action makes the other person feel comfortable?

So let's translate that idea to an audience. We have to build a relationship with audiences larger than one. Reading the audience plus the Platinum Rule might look like this: If you're coming on very loud and strong in a small, quiet room, the audience may feel overwhelmed. They might sit back, look down, or turn their bodies to the side. Watch for clues that you need to ease into your presentation to pull them out of their shell slowly. Or maybe they've been watching boring slides for an hour and are slumped in their chairs. That's an indication to turn up the heat and wake them up.

Reading an audience involves a lot of attention, some intuition, and practice. You'll become better and better at assessing and managing your audience the more you present. So be patient, present as often as you can, and keep the focus outward.

STINKY ROOMS—WHY ENVIRONMENT MATTERS SO MUCH

Think about the absolutely worst room you've ever been in for a presentation. What made it stink? A hot, cramped space; an uncomfortable chair; and you were way in the back and couldn't see the screen, plus there was no microphone, so you couldn't really hear what was going on, and it may have, literally, stunk. I've been in more smelly, dirty, windowless rooms crammed with unnecessary junk than I can count. That environment made it almost impossible for me to concentrate on the presenter.

So what do you do if you have to present in a rotten room? Everything you possibly can.

You have the right to take complete responsibility for the

environment. Whether it's a meeting room, a dining room, or a coliseum, it's your stage! We don't realize how much clutter, dirtiness, or unneeded paraphernalia can derail our focus. You may be tempted to say, "Well, Facilities was supposed to set up the room differently. Oh, well." Don't do it! I have rallied help more times than I can count to improve the environment and comfort of my audience. I've moved more tables and chairs, cleaned up more trash, adjusted more lighting, and wound more power cords in my life than a roadie for Lady Gaga. If no break is scheduled right before my speech, I work with the organizers to schedule one. If the room is dark, I turn up the lights and open curtains. A bright room is an awake room. I've changed thermostats, called for fans, and opened or closed windows and doors. You can, too.

I was once right in the middle of a speech in El Paso, Texas, for the Young Presidents Organization, when I realized that I was getting really hot. I could see one man near the front with sweat actually dripping from his brow. I noticed for the first time that the facility staff had closed every window and door for my speech. When I asked if anyone else was uncomfortable, the whole audience concurred, whistling and waving their programs. We couldn't find any staff (isn't it amazing how they always disappear just when you need 'em?), so I enlisted a few gentlemen to help me prop open doors and windows. Fresh, cool air blew in—ahhhh! No one minded the interruption—we were all just happy to be cool again.

I always get to my venue early, and some of the things I check out include:

> How big is the room? How many people will be in it?

> Are the seats set so that everyone can see?

› Where will I stand? How will I move around so that every-one can see me and I them?

› Cords! Where are they, can we get them taped down, and how do I keep my big Bozo feet from tripping over them?

› Where are the light switches?

› What's the noise level in the space? Will we be able to hear external sounds?

› And, most important, who can help me? Can I rally strong people to help me rearrange chairs? Is this a union facility? Do I need to make requests in advance?

Let me tell you, I'm a demanding woman about the envi-ronment. And I'm not about to apologize because it completely affects an audience's enjoyment of a fabulously bad presentation. You'll probably be nicer.

Here are two examples I can just never get over. I really look forward to being in an audience or being an attendee of a meet-ing, especially if there's going to be a professional presenter or facilitator. I figure I can relax and just be a participant.

I had a "professional" facilitator who was the most solid exam-ple of mediocre in history. She did not greet us and show us to our seats at the first meeting. We had to search through the table tents, and only half the names were turned out (as they should have been, so that fellow meeting participants could read them), while half remained turned toward the attendee. She never fixed that, although people commented on how confusing it was. Her flip charts were small, low, and unreadable. I mentioned that her markers were worn out and we couldn't see the lettering. She laughed and said, "Oh this room always has the worst markers!"

As I walked away, all I could think about was the office supply store in the downstairs lobby where a three dollar purchase could have solved the issue. The food servers left nowhere for us to bus our dirty dishes. Twenty-five people were politely trying to clear the work area, and the situation was not rectified in the three days of our meeting.

When I entered the room on the second day, it was in disarray. Trash was all over the tables, notes were scattered about, and chairs were rolled everywhere. As a participant, I expected to enter a room fresh and ready to begin again. The facilitator sat at her table sipping coffee and reading the newspaper.

Ugh. I know. Stop now before you burst a vein, lady.

As a presenter, a member of a meeting, or a facilitator, you have a right to speak with anyone whose work affects your event. Go out and find the people who should supply cleanup, and if they cannot help, go get a tray yourself. Bring your own supplies if you can't trust a location to provide them, and listen to the needs of your audience.

Hang on. I'm just getting warmed up. Here's another example.

Once I came into a room with an experienced speaker with whom I was copresenting, only to find a disaster. All the chairs were stacked; it was after hours, so no facilities personnel were there, and our audience was due to arrive in forty-five minutes. He told me, "I don't move chairs. I've been doing this for fifteen years—moving chairs is not part of my job description." As I controlled the urge to strangle him, I decided to ask a question instead.

ME: Who will move them?

HIM: We'll tell the audience to grab a chair when they get here.

ME: We're presenting to one hundred senior citizens and home health-care professionals on generational differences. What happens when most of our audience isn't capable of moving a chair?

HIM: Well, I'll help then.

ME: Who else of importance is coming tonight?

HIM: The CEO of the largest senior-care system in the US. I believe he'll want to buy our services.

ME: How impressed will he be when we ask him to move his own chair, our presentation begins thirty minutes late, and he watches us do nothing while little old ladies drag chairs around?

He finally shut up and helped me move the chairs.

Over the top? Maybe. You're a busy person. How many times have you been in a room where you were distracted, uncomfortable, or unable to hear or see and wished you could just get out? The more you can alleviate these discomforts and create a place where people can breathe easily and focus on the message, the more effective your presentation will be. Environment is the ultimate example of focusing on your audience rather than yourself —which actually makes you more successful.

WHAT ABOUT HECKLERS?

I know that I just said that audiences really want you to do well. That's true 99 percent of the time. Unless you are a politician or a comedian, and then you've just painted a target on your chest.

Let's talk about the rare occasion when you might have to deal with hecklers. I worked with a woman who had to manage crises in the field for construction companies. If something went wrong or there was a safety citation, it was her job to go out and discuss it with the on-site crews. In addition to the stress of the situations, she also had to deal with obvious gender imbalances. More often than not, she was the only woman in the room dealing with very angry or upset construction workers. It was intimidating to say the least.

We worked on using the tools at her command to change the energy in the room. If someone spoke loudly and quickly to her, she responded in the low, slow voice we had practiced. If someone was using a negative, low, slow delivery, she responded with direct eye contact and a high, energetic voice and a concise answer. By counteracting the negative delivery of the attacker, she was able to balance the energy of the room. This simple change made a huge difference for her. Instead of responding in kind and escalating the intensity of the conversation, she was able to diffuse a lot of emotion by balancing the conversation. It lent authority to her presence and allowed her to remain in control.

I also work with a global food company that has a rather harsh culture. The employees dread visits from headquarters. They relate stories of being interrupted with abrupt questions and being told they are not presenting the right information and to sit down. Cringe! For those situations, being released from the rules of presenting is a huge relief. Rather than going blank on a harsh question or feeling the pressure to answer, you should practice the art of replying to the attacker with an open-ended question: "Tell me more about your concern. What are your thoughts on this issue?" If you can get the attacker to speak again, you'll obtain more information about their concerns and have time to breathe and gather yourself.

You can also take away an attacker's ammunition. If you know there's a problem brewing, address it first. If you know, say, that a research project didn't go as planned, don't avoid the topic; bring it up yourself so that a heckler doesn't have to. Doing this disarms any hecklers and affirms that you're willing to handle the tough stuff head on.

You can also put any hecklers in the parking lot. Answer their initial question, but if they continue to press, let them know that you honor their question but need to stay on track for the good of the whole audience. Smile really convincingly and say something like, "I hear your concern. What I'd like to do is speak to you right after the end of the speech. There are a lot of people here, and I want to respect their time commitment. Please meet me at the side of the stage afterward, and I'll be glad to address your concerns."

"You big fat dork." (That part is in your head. Don't say it out loud.)

Finally, I always recommend the high road. (This from a woman who calls people names in her head.) An anonymous source once said, "Don't wrestle with pigs. You both get dirty, and the pig likes it." If you don't have an answer or need more time, you can be honest. Just say, "I can get a complete answer for you —let's arrange a different time to connect."

Now let's look at the most extreme example of heckling. A member of my company ensemble, Jason, is a stand-up comedian. And despite his willingness to dive into the mud pit, he's had to learn some hard lessons about dealing with tough audiences. Granted, stand-up is a different beast from what most of us will ever deal with—comics actually choose to stroll into a snake pit of drunken audiences. But Jason's story really exemplifies the need to figure out what's right for you.

I remember the first time I was seriously heckled. I tried to shout the heckler down, but it backfired. I got angry. He got angry. The audience turned on me. And I bombed.

Backstage, a great, seasoned comedienne pulled me aside. She told me that I had to find a way to grab control of my performance, but that would mean involving the heckler. That sounded counterintuitive and counterproductive. But I gave it a shot. The next time I got heckled, I asked the heckler where he was from and then made a joke about that. I got him and the audience laughing. I came out smelling like a rose. Now, I even look forward to hecklers so that I can improvise with them.

So why did the audience turn on Jason the first time? He's a clever guy with a cutting tongue. When he shamed the heckler, they were embarrassed and began to side with their coaudience member. In contrast, by leaning on his colleague's advice and engaging the next heckler in a playful way, Jason kept the audience on the comic's side. In other words, show up the heckler but don't eviscerate him.

Now let's not be naïve. The job of many comics *is* to insult the audience. Ironically, Jason got the opposite advice from another comic a year later. Jason had dealt with a heckler in a show, and the audience sided with him happily. The second comic told him to never let a heckler off the hook—that he should have slammed him, insulted him, and beat him down. In the end, it's a stylistic choice, and the playful approach worked better for Jason. I also believe that this is the single best choice for presenters—playful, respectful, and straightforward.

One last note: the world of professional stand-up comedy is a far cry from the effective presentations we are talking about in this book. But we can learn from it. We can learn from every example of a person attempting to influence an audience. And the beauty of Jason's stories is that comics understand their badness. They embrace the fact that they're there to break rules— to surprise, engage, and stimulate their audience. I'll bet almost every comic on the planet has the same purpose. Get out there and kill it: make the audience laugh so hard they can't breathe. And do it with focus, passion, and purpose.

For a short video on Audience,
visit www.ImprovEdge.com/videos

TWO

YOU ARE THE PRESENTATION

So Be Your Baddest You

We all refer to presentations in the third person, as though they were objects: "Send the presentation to Marketing" or "Post the presentation to the intranet."

This assumes that the presentation is the PowerPoint file, the technology, the content. But guess what? The real presentation is you. *You* are the one who can make all of those mere props— PowerPoint slides, flip charts, pictures—come to life and have meaning. A slide deck without a person isn't a presentation. It's a document. So, if Marketing really wants the presentation sent over to them, you should just mail yourself in a manila envelope.

Do you think actors wait until the set, costumes, and props are in place before they rehearse or decide how their characters feel? Heavens, no. The acting and directing ensemble figures out what they want to accomplish—and the accouterments of the show support those decisions. The key here for presenters is to achieve real impact and get away from useless props.

So here are some ideas to unlock the baddest you.

Be a first-rate version of yourself, not a second-rate version of someone else.

—*Judy Garland*

#5: Open with your introduction and close with questions

Like a dreaded college lecturer? Bookends will hook your audience and send them out singing!

Bookends. Those solid pieces of wood or marble that keep your library shelf intact and your books upright. They're strong, they're reliable, and they can't be ignored. When your presentation has bookends, your audience knows you mean business. Grab their attention immediately when you arrive onstage. Then send them out with a bang.

Bookends are critical to audience perception because of *recency* and *primacy*. These concepts mean that the first thing people hear is memorable, and, after a lot of interim information, the last thing they hear sticks too.[1] Your job is to make both matter.

THE HOOK

If you want a hook to work, it's got to be interesting. Your fish, the audience, won't bite and be reeled in unless something really tasty grabs its attention. How's this for a completely empty hook?

"Good afternoon, I'm Karen. I'm here to talk about the steps for completing an expense report. I'll be covering six steps for expense reports. Let's go to the first slide."

Have you ever heard a presentation begin this way? And what happened? You got bored, lost interest, or even felt embarrassed for the presenter if she seemed nervous or stumbled. Even when a presenter gives a crisp introduction, you're still probably unimpressed. That's because you expected it: greeting, name, and topic. Standard. Boring. No enticing, wiggly worm.

Why is this so important? Researchers at New York University have shown that people form opinions of others within the first seven to thirty seconds. The reason our assessments are formed so quickly is based on survival: the structure of the brain is ancient, and we still have many of the same neural processes our ancestors did. For example, they had to be able to instantly assess whether new people were safe or dangerous; the speed of this decision could mean life or death. Those instincts in the ancient areas of our brains are still active and now apply to social situations. In as little as seven seconds, we decide how we instinctually feel about someone: our brain assesses a person's dress, smile, energy, confidence, and posture, and it then makes a snap decision about the person's level of education, trustworthiness, and intellect.[2]

Those fascinating findings are connected to other research on trust and generosity. Not only do others make decisions about you, their decisions can be affected by how you choose to interact with them first. Paul J. Zak found that social interactions with strangers could boost or lower the oxytocin levels in the participants of his study. Oxytocin is a chemical found in both men and women, although it is most recognized as a hormone present during childbirth and labor. Again, our ancient brains assess strangers as we encounter them, making immediate decisions about whether we're safe to trust them. If we feel we can trust them, our oxytocin level rises. If they make us feel unsafe, or if we intrinsically do not trust them, our oxytocin level lowers. But here's the kicker: when a stranger is generous, kind, or shows trust toward you, you're more likely to trust them back. In other words, first behaviors of other people toward you can actually affect how your body reacts and whether your brain decides to trust them.[3]

How can we build trust, connections, and anticipation with our audiences? Consider the first moment of impact. You want to grab your listeners' attention, surprise them, engage them, challenge them. Think about what you want to convey, and try as many different openings as you can—the more you have in your pocket, the more often you can make the most of that vital first impression.

You could use a rhetorical question with a startling fact: "Did you know that 22 million people in the US suffer from some sort of hearing loss? And hearing disabilities are found in all age groups! I'm Chris, and I'm here to talk about the use of hearing devices."

You could engage the audience: "Please raise your hand if you ate breakfast this morning. Wow, only about a third of you! My name is Anita, and my research proves that a good breakfast is the most important part of losing excess weight."

You could surprise them by entering from the back of the room—yelling, or singing, or juggling. It would certainly make them curious as to what's coming next.

On January 6, 1941, Franklin D. Roosevelt opened his State of the Union address with these powerful lines:

> Mr. Speaker, members of the Seventy-Seventh Congress:
> I address you, the members of the Seventy-Seventh Congress, at a moment unprecedented in the history of the Union. I use the word "unprecedented" because at no

previous time has American security been as seriously threatened from without as it is today.[4]

His hook made it clear that this was a seminal moment in history and that everyone in that room had a vital part in it.

On the flip side of that coin, I've seen a few pros really botch their openings. One professional, paid speaker at a conference had a very impressive video introduction. It included music, a professional voiceover, clips of her on TV shows, and a high-energy vibe. Everyone was completely pumped to see her arrive onstage. After that gigantic windup, she wandered onstage, and in a small voice said something like, "You know when you don't know what to say in a presentation?" She meandered around a little and finally whispered that we'd be hearing her stories of presenting. Are you kidding? It was the letdown of the century.

I also once saw a celebrity from a 1980s sitcom speak, and he barely hit mediocre. I think he might have spent two minutes on the plane ride realizing that he was about to give a speech. He stepped onstage, after a huge introduction about how amazing his career was and how wonderful he was going to be. He then did not two, not three, but four false starts. It sounded something like this: "So I thought I'd tell you… um…. I mean when I was a… so… it's just kids sometimes…. The sitcom helped me hit it big, but I… so anyway, it's great to be here at your luncheon." It's exhausting just thinking about how unprepared he was. I was ticked off, too. He was being paid big bucks by a charity I love to be the speaker for the annual fundraiser. After blowing the opening, he strung together a bunch of unrelated stories and weakly tried to tie it to the mission of the organization. Yuck.

You are so much better than that! Just think, with a little preparation and creativity, you could probably blow me or any professional out of the water with your bad, beautiful hook. Your hook tells the audience that this is not going to be an ordinary presentation. It's going to be interesting, different, engaging. And it sets the mood for the entire presentation.

APOLOGIZING AND CRAMMING

Apologizing for your flaws, especially in the first few sentences, is like a hook with a sign that says "I'm going to drag you to your death." So many presenters open with an apology: "Um, I'm not very good at this. Sorry, I didn't have much time to prepare."

Your audience isn't likely to notice your flaws. If they do, they'll overlook them if you show a genuine respect for both the audience and your topic. Why would you say you're a terrible presenter, that you're not prepared, that you're nervous, or that you heard about giving this presentation only yesterday? We can't tell if you don't tell us.

Besides, your flaws may be the energy and passion that make you bad in the best way. Don't apologize for being you—that's what we're here for.

Openings also suffer when you tell the audience they're about to drink from a fire hose. How do you feel when a presenter says, "I'm sorry, I have to rush and cram four hours of information into one hour for my presentation because they didn't give me enough time"? Maybe cheated or confused, as the presenter zooms through too much? If a group has asked you to speak for a certain period of time, you should consider that a compliment. Anyone who takes the time to hear your hour-long speech wants to receive value for that time commitment. They won't care that you normally deliver your speech in a four-hour workshop. If you just keep repeating how much better the four-hour version is, zoom through ridiculous amounts of information, and show no effort to deliver a succinct message, it will annoy your listeners. Four hours obviously will not fit into one. So take the time to edit, choose a simple purpose, and deliver value for an hour. If you're good, people will come back for more the next time.

That concept also holds true for the wrap-it-up moment. Have you ever seen a speaker get "the sign"? That's when someone off-stage lets the speaker know that time is running out. Suddenly they speed up. Their eyes widen, they begin to cram as many words, concepts, and slides into the final minute as they can, and —you got it—they apologize. It's like an apology cram sandwich. "Wow, I have only two minutes left?! Oh, sorry everybody, guess I wasn't keeping track of time. Okay, no worries. I'll cover these last twenty-three bullets and get you all out of here!"

When you are short on time, edit rather than cram. If you suddenly have only two minutes left, that's a great moment to take a breath and slow down. In your head, you can prioritize. Of those twenty-three final bullets, which ones are really critical? You can probably cover only two, so choose them. Or consider ditching the last bullets, remind the audience of the important points you've already covered, and give them a bang-up close.

Je n'ai fait celle-ci plus longue que parce que je n'ai pas eu le loisir de la faire plus courte.

(**I have made this** [letter] **longer than usual because I have not had time to make it shorter.**)

—*Blaise Pascal*

SEND THEM OUT SINGING

This is a classic rule from musical theater. Have you ever noticed that great musicals always end on a powerful or upbeat song that sticks in your head? That's because composers and lyricists want to send the audience out singing their songs. They want hundreds of raving fans for their plays taking the message and music out to other ticket buyers.

You too want to leave your audience with a sticky, compelling message. You grabbed them early on with a hook, you used purpose and action to move them, and now you need to close with a bang.

Summarize the information you really want the audience to remember. If songs have refrains, so also can speeches. In fact, retention increases over the long term when adults are presented with information multiple times.[5] Use the power of repetition to teach the audience your main points.

Tell the audience what you are going to say, then say it, then tell them what you've said.

—Dale Carnegie

Your closing statement could include a memorable statement or a call to action. John F. Kennedy did this in his inaugural address on January 20, 1961:

> And so, my fellow Americans: ask not what your country can do for you—ask what you can do for your country. My fellow citizens of the world: ask not what America will do for you, but what together we can do for the freedom of Man.[6]

Martin Luther King also did this in his famous "I Have a Dream" speech in 1963:

> When we let freedom ring—when we let it ring from every village and every hamlet, from every state and every city, we will be able to speed up that day when all of God's children—black men and white men, Jews and Gentiles, Protestants and Catholics—will be able to join hands and sing in the words of the old Negro spiritual: "Free at last! Free at last! Thank God Almighty, we are free at last!"[7]

Every time I hear a recording of those final moments of King's speech, my skin tingles and my heart leaps. You also can bring power to the final moments of your presentation. What do you want to leave with your audience?

This is why I never end on questions. Visualize a standard Q&A session. After the questions have petered out, you or maybe a moderator thank the audience and you walk away. It's a weak closing. The audience might remember the last question you answered. It might have been a good answer. It might have been a weak answer. Either way, the Q&A time steals your thunder. Always have a back-pocket closer with which to send your audience out singing.

Try handling it this way—when the questions are done, control the close. Give them a call to action—"Thanks for your questions. Remember, commit to eating a full breakfast every morning. You'll lose weight and gain brain power for a better you! Thank you, everyone!"—and walk off the stage.

Or how about this? "I appreciate your questions. Vote to uphold our parks tomorrow. If it weren't for the city park near my childhood home, I never would have played sports or been a coach today. It's the best thing in my life, and I owe it to a city park. Please vote!"

Send them out singing, and they'll be back the next time you put on a show.

**For a short video on Bookends,
visit www.ImprovEdge.com/videos**

#6: You either have confidence or you don't

That's bogus. You can teach your body confidence. And your body is your most powerful tool.

If I asked you to walk around a room as though you were the most confident person in the world—if I asked you to show me confidence, only with your body and without words—what would it look like? You might stand up straight and walk slowly with long strides and smooth arm gestures. You'd look people in the eye, smile, and hold up your chin. You would breathe deeply, and your shoulders would relax.

If I then asked you to walk around showing me the physical manifestation of fear and nervousness, you would probably close in on yourself. You might hold your arms tightly to your body, duck your head, move erratically and quickly, as though fearing danger at any moment. Your eyes would dart around, and your breathing would be fast and shallow.

Try it out now: get up from your seat and walk around the room first in confidence and then in fear. Note how different you feel, and how your body tries to *show* those emotions.

This nonverbal exercise has an important purpose. We have a misconception that presentations are about the words that we say and the slides we show. Presentations are actually all about what we do with our bodies. People focus on your body, usually without even realizing it. Much more impact comes from your body than from your words. As a matter of fact, putting your body into expansive, powerful poses can actually create confidence.

Confidence is a doozy of a concern for a huge percentage of people—whether they present formally to crowds or just to small groups at weekly meetings. People often say gaining confidence is their biggest goal.

Get ready. You have the instant ability to do just that. All you have to do is make your body look confident. When William James said, "Act as if you are beautiful, confident and poised, and you will be,"[8] he was more right than he might have realized. The way you hold your body can actually change the level of power and confidence you feel.

We all have attitudes and perspectives within us that come alive from body cues, not from mindsets. In fact, those who study the psychology of self-efficacy (your belief in your ability to perform a certain task or skill) have found that one key to unlocking confidence is to talk your body into it, even before your mind. For example, if you show the physical signs of happiness (smiling), you will feel happier. Your face, body, and voice send signals to your brain, informing it that you are experiencing a particular emotion because you are engaging in behaviors that signal happiness. You then feel that emotion.

One study even showed that forcing the body to change can affect mood and attitude. In 2006, ten clinically depressed patients, who had been depressed for between two and ten years and who had not responded to drug therapy, were administered a drug that reduced their frown lines. In other words, researchers used Botox to force the patients' faces to assume a happier aspect—free of frown lines and down expressions. Two months later, without additional drugs, nine of the ten were no longer depressed.[9] And no, silly, I'm not telling you to go get Botox. The point is that by forcing the patients' bodies to send new signals to their brains, their chemical depression began to improve. This astonishing finding is only the beginning.

Some of the most fascinating research in this arena comes from Amy J.C. Cuddy, as reported by the Harvard Business School. In her work, "Power Posing: Brief Nonverbal Displays Affect Neuroendocrine Levels and Risk Tolerance,"[10] she illuminates the fact that we have much more ability to manipulate our confidence than we realize. Cuddy and her coauthors conducted experiments to measure several important hormones. The first was testosterone, which is present in both the human and animal worlds and correlates with greater confidence, risk tolerance, power, and dominance when it is present in the body at higher levels. The second was cortisol, a hormone that's present in the brain and body during times of stress, fear, and lack of confidence and which can also over time create hypertension and memory loss.

In her experiments, Cuddy's subjects were asked to hold high-power, expansive poses—such as putting their feet on a desk with their hands behind their head—for one to two minutes. Members of another control group were directed to sit with their legs crossed and their arms protecting their bodies, often with their heads down. Saliva samples from before and after the experiment showed astonishing changes. Controlling for the subjects' baseline levels of both hormones, Cuddy and her coauthors found that high-power poses decreased cortisol by about 25 percent and increased testosterone by about 19 percent in both men and women. By contrast, the low-power poses increased cortisol about 17 percent and decreased testosterone about 10 percent.

In addition, the people who had taken on the high-power poses said they felt very "in charge" and "powerful." They felt confident. This research has ramifications not only for presentations but for anyone who might feel powerless or have low self-esteem. By manipulating the way you hold your body, you can affect your level of confidence and sense of control. And by managing your internal confidence, by building yourself up and giving yourself more power, you in turn affect how your audience feels about you.

My geek core gets so worked up about this stuff! By changing our bodies, we control chemicals that can affect our confidence. When we are positive, confident, and willing to make a warm connection with our audience, they will respond. As Cuddy elaborates:

> We are influenced, and influence others, through very unconscious and implicit processes. People tend to spend too much energy focusing on the words they're saying—perfectly crafting the content of the message—when in many cases that matters much less than how it's being communicated. People often are more influenced by how they feel about you than by what you're saying. It's not about the content of the message, but how you're communicating it.[11]

I've learned that people will forget what you said, people will forget what you did, but people will never forget how you made them feel.

—Maya Angelou

WHAT IS YOUR BODY REALLY SAYING?

But wait—there's more. Dr. Albert Mehrabian, a psychologist and professor at UCLA, tells us about the importance of nonverbal communication. Mehrabian was interested in the impact of verbal and nonverbal communication on our impressions of each other—how we decide whether we like another person. He was really curious about the effect of inconsistent messages (like saying yes although your arms are crossed and your body is tight, which nonverbally indicates no). The study found that in deciding whether we like someone, body language (visual and total body picture) is worth 55 percent of our decision.[12]

But what else mattered? Mehrabian also determined that tone of voice (vocal) is 38 percent of the reason we decide to like someone else. Call-center professionals know this only too well. In a company I work with, they have a phrase called "poor voice." If someone arrives at work after an argument, if they were especially stressed, they might have trouble calming their voice before getting on the phone. That could kill sales. If the employee can't calm down and control his tone, he might be sent home.

So that leaves us with 7 percent. What's left? Words. Only 7 percent of our total decision whether to like someone is based on the words they say. Let's be clear: This study isn't a generalization about the impact of all communication. Email does not convey only 7 percent of a message, and you can't watch a person speaking in a foreign language and understand 93 percent. But its findings are useful if we think about the study in a larger sense. Put simply, it's not just about our words. Without nonverbal indicators, it's easier to misunderstand the words.

Think about email. It strips away 93 percent of our ability to influence how people understand our message. How many times have you been offended by an email? Or worse, how many times have you sent an email, meant no harm whatsoever, and the message was taken totally wrong on the other end?! This overused form of communication has started to replace authentic interaction. It's a good tool that has grown horns and teeth. When you have an important message and can pick up the phone (adding your tone of voice to clarify meaning) or can walk down the hall and speak in person (adding your confident body language to the message), do it. Use the human tools at your disposal whenever possible.

So how do these three elements come together? When we feel that a person is not telling the truth, we intuitively check out the alignment between words, voice, and body. When you want someone to trust you, check out the alignment between your own words, voice, and body because if they aren't in sync, the observer is likely to rely on your body language. It's just like watching people say to their significant other, "Sure honey, go ahead with your friends and have a good time," but their arms are crossed, their faces are mad, and their tone of voice is screaming "Don't you dare go out tonight!"

So what does this mean for us as presenters? We have to come to grips with the fact that feeling confident and managing our body is a priority if we're going to be truly bad. If you change anything about your work as a presenter, make intentional choices about what your body is saying.

**Everything you want is just outside
your comfort zone.**

—*Robert Allen*

INTENTIONAL BODY LANGUAGE

Try thinking of your body as a tool for impact. For starters, is there a particularly important point in your presentation that you want to be sure people remember? Pair the importance of the message with the movement of your body. If you've been stand-ing in one place, move all the way across the stage and stand right next to your audience when you hit the key point. Or have you been casually moving around during your presentation? When you get to that critical moment, plant your feet, become very still, and deliver very clearly. Surprise your audience by changing the rhythm, location, speed, or power of your movements.

Try experimenting with movement. Just figure that you're going to feel a bit goofy at first. Engage in the confidence/fear exercise I described at the start of this chapter. Find out what it feels like to exaggerate your movements—to act supremely confi-dent, terribly scared, sad, or excited. What happens to your body when you take on those emotions? How is it "speaking?" Then explore options for moving around the stage. If you tend to get stuck in one position, travel the stage from edge to edge. If you're a mover, see what sort of impact you can create with stillness. And just do what feels right to you. Stretch your comfort zone a bit, and you'll be surprised at the wonderful new ways you begin to connect with your audience.

Abraham Lincoln stood absolutely still, straight, and quiet; he never touched the podium, never made wild gestures, and never walked around. Conversely, Theodore Roosevelt was a fiery speaker who used his whole body as an instrument of expression. It was often said that sweat and spittle flew off his body. Both Lincoln and Roosevelt were being themselves, and they were both excellent speakers with lots of impact. Their natural body expressions became an extension and a carrier of their message; full of gravitas or full of fire.

I once read an article that absolutely insisted that you anchor yourself to the audience's left side of the screen. It went on to explain how that allowed the audience to read your slides without distraction. The irony was that this section of the article was titled "Communication Is Mostly Physical." It almost made my eyes hurt to read it. It paid tribute to the importance of physicality, and in the next sentence put a weight around the neck of every presenter, reiterating that the audience reading the slides was more important than the audience looking at the person.

Being stuck next to the screen is a very common issue we encounter—because of rules! Sometimes people feel safer if they are farther from the audience. Whenever I ask volunteers to join me on stage for a speech or an improvisational game, there's a "drift" that begins almost immediately. They arrive on stage, excited and smiling, take one look at the audience, and unconsciously begin to step back. I've had to keep a hand behind the backs of some volunteers to keep them from smacking into the rear wall.

I understand. The unconscious need for space increases exponentially onstage. Ever heard of "personal space"? Depending on your culture, a certain space feels right and comfortable for people to stand in to have a conversation. When you encounter someone who has a different unconscious "personal space," you can feel really uncomfortable. Have you ever talked with someone who was just a little too close? And when you took a tiny step back to get a little breathing room, the person just moved in again?

I once worked with a group of scientists on perfecting their introductions and networking skills. One very tall, rather awkward gentleman was in a role-playing exercise with me about introducing yourself to a stranger. He towered over me and just kept moving in closer, no matter how much I tried to show that I was uncomfortable with his approach. I was using my acting skills to try to give him the hint, and finally his colleagues—the audience—cracked up laughing. They were trying to hold it in, but the scene was filled with the comedy of discomfort. The point was that the poor man was oblivious. He didn't realize how intimidating his height could be or that his physical proximity was getting in the way of making easy connections with new people.

And in the same way, we've become used to stage space. Over the centuries, there has always been a big space between the people on stage and the audience. But here's the problem—this space makes it much harder to connect with your audience. It's the opposite problem I encountered with the scientist. He was too close, but the stage is usually putting us too far away. You've got to learn how it feels to stand close to people, how to move up into the light at the lip of the stage or speaking area. For one thing, you never know when you'll be working in a cramped space. You might have to stand right next to the front row, so you might as well practice it now.

How do you stay relaxed? Are you aware of your stature—how can you make the audience feel comfortable with that proximity? How do you make eye contact with people in the back as well as those at the front? How do you find a way to move a bit and alter your total body picture, even if you've only got a few square feet to work with? These are the kinds of issues to explore with your body in practice.

Here's another favorite issue: "What do I do with my hands?" The answer is simple. Just let them hang on the ends of your wrists until you can't keep them still. In other words, you shouldn't plan or formalize your gestures. They should flow naturally from your instincts, your topic—from YOU!

My company once worked with a participant who really struggled with breaking those rules. He'd been to so many presentation-skills classes, he was convinced that the rules were inviolable. But his presentations were stilted and stiff. For example, he kept his right hand practically pasted to his thigh and only gestured with his left—it looked really weird. When we discussed the issue, he said, "I was taught to put my hand against my cell phone inside my pocket to keep it from wandering." But the issue was not his hand movements, the issue was the rule. Once he unglued his hand from his side, we could focus on him and not his strange stance.

You can also be intentional about building up your confidence in external ways. If you like to feel polished and dressed up, more power to you. When I was performing improv at Yale, we teased one of our ensemble members, Frances, about her boots. She wore them for every show. They were sturdy, made her feel grounded, and inspired her to choose strong, badass characters. Don't underestimate the importance of making yourself feel great. A professional speaker once told me that when she speaks, she always wears something given to her by someone who loves her. It gives her courage and reminds her of what matters.

A friend once told me that this research on body confidence fills him with memories of his basic training for the US Army. That training teaches men and women to stand up straight, hold their heads high, and attain the posture of confidence. That constant training helps them become soldiers—people who are actually courageous enough to go into battle. You can usually spot military personnel if they are out of uniform—their confidence gives them away.

DISABILITIES

What about people who don't have full control of their bodies? How do these ideas apply to people bound to a wheelchair, to amputees, or to those with other physical issues? First of all, understand that whatever your total body picture might be, it's a striking part of your delivery, of who you are, and it is a strength, not a weakness. I am fortunate to have full body control and am grateful every day for that blessing. I can say, however, that a few of the most impressive speakers I've ever seen had disabilities and used them in an intentional way to create power in their presentations.

I remember watching a professional speaker who happened to be wheelchair bound. She ignored every so-called limitation and gave an inspiring, incredible speech. She used her voice, face, and arms to their full capacity—and she used the entire stage by moving her wheelchair around to get closer to and connect with audience members. Then, in a delightful moment, she invited an audience member up on stage with her to wheel her around. Volunteer hands shot up. She chose a gentleman, told him where to push her wheelchair, and had him use his own legs to demonstrate concepts.

This American Life, the NPR radio show, featured writer David Rakoff in a special episode that was staged live and beamed to theaters all over the country. The deterioration of Rakoff's body because of an illness was the subject of his speech. He talked about his love of dance, intertwining the story of his body's slow decline and the eventual loss of the use of his arm. But the most incredible and beautiful moment of the speech was when he stopped speaking and began to dance. It was not his words or his disability or his useless limb that drew attention, but the graceful and beautiful power of the way he used his body despite its limitations.[13]

Helen Keller, though blind and deaf as a result of a childhood disease, became a world-renowned speaker and author. She found ways to communicate to audiences through sign language, spoken words, and interpretation. Her disabilities were her strengths, and she continually found ways to share her life and views as fully as any other person.

When I graduated from Yale, Stephen Hawking, the famous physicist who has no motor capabilities because he has the degenerative disease ALS, received an honorary degree. On TV, he once commented about how his brilliant and breakthrough theories in physics might never have come to light had his body not been disabled. He considered his disease an invitation for his mind to soar. I remember him up on the stage. I can say first-hand his body had a huge impact—his very stillness was striking and meaningful.

SMALL BUT MIGHTY

One last story: I once worked with an executive team from a global media company that creates news and entertainment on television and digital channels around the world. One of the executives was a woman from the United Kingdom. She was barely five feet tall, but she filled the area around her with energy and confidence. She smiled and laughed often, was wickedly smart, and knew how to engage an individual or a room. In the class, when we came to the section on using your body effectively, she shared a story. Her petite English mother had raised a family of petite daughters, all just like the executive. However, this mother could make anything happen and never let her stature get in her way. Whenever one of them was heading out of the house or had a challenge to face, she would tell them the same thing: "Chin up. Chest out. Lipstick on."

Amazing—no wonder this executive had such a big presence! From the time she was a girl, she learned that she could face anything with the right physicality. Mum was right.

**For a short video on Confidence,
visit www.ImprovEdge.com/videos**

#7: What you say is most important

It's *how* you say it
that matters.

Picture a professional athlete—strong, tough, competitive. Now hear the sound in your head of a professional opera singer—strong, melodic, powerful. Do you think either one heads out to perform without warming up? Do you think they would even consider going out to play or perform by just rolling out of their car and onto the field or stage? Not a chance. I've noticed throughout my career that it's only the amateurs who think they can wing it, who believe it's beneath them to prepare. The great presenters, salespeople, executives, actors, and athletes? They all prepare and warm up.

So let's talk about a tool at your disposal as a speaker: your voice. High performers in any field take time to train and develop the tools they have. Bringing your consciousness to your voice will help you use it effectively and strategically. After all, being understood—by our audiences, our teams, our direct reports, and our spouses—is our responsibility.

Consider your audience. There's nothing more frustrating to an audience than not being able to properly hear or understand a presenter. I remember seeing a highly paid speaker in Las Vegas at a conference. She was a famous poker player and had a great persona and an interesting story. Too bad we missed most of it. She slurred, mumbled, and spoke very quickly. I lost about every tenth word in spite of her microphone. The whole audience was frustrated simply because we were straining to understand her words.

So remember—my job here is to nudge you out of your comfort zone. Try something completely different. It might make a monumental difference. And if it makes you even a little better, and a little badder, isn't it worth a try?

WHAT'S IN A VOICE?

The Vegas speaker had a mike, but it didn't matter. She did not know how to use her voice. Your voice has quite a number of elements:

> Articulation—Clarity of pronunciation

> Pitch—High and low tones

> Volume—Loudness or softness of speech

> Timbre—The quality and type of sound the voice makes

> Speed—Fast or slow pacing

> Connection to breath—The amount of air that carries the sound

> Silence

Let me grab my Follow Me, I'm Your Tour Guide sign, and I'll walk you through these attributes of your voice.

Articulation is key to being heard and understood. In general, you can improve your articulation by improving your ability to project clear consonants. The tongue is the hardest worker, a group of muscles continually in motion. Three primary areas of the mouth work with your tongue to create sounds for consonants. The lips (make the sounds *puh* or *buh* to feel the lips), the hard ridge behind the teeth (say *tee* or *dee*), and the back of the roof of the mouth (say *kuh* or *guh*).

To warm up, repeat those sounds and pay attention to those areas. Next, try a few more tricks of the trade to get your articulators ready: Stretch your face out. Chew a big imaginary wad of gum. Move your lips and jaw around. Imagine you have very sticky peanut butter all over your teeth, and work aggressively to remove it. Much like an athlete practices drills or a musician practices scales, exercises like these are great practices for presenters.

And yes, we all look stupid when we do this. So do it in the car, or in your office facing away from the glass. Stretching out your tongue and face, rolling through *Tuh, tuh, buh, buh, guh, guh* a few times won't kill you, and you'll speak far more clearly with just sixty seconds of warm-up.

Pitch keeps us from the dreaded monotone. One way to grab your audience is to change the pitch of your voice. If you're saying something humorous, your pitch is likely to be high. If you're saying something serious, use a pitch that's low. As a woman, I've carefully lowered my pitch in important situations. People can unconsciously discount high voices because they trigger the sense that you're talking to a younger person. We subconsciously associate authority with a lower pitch.

Volume is the amount of sound you can project, and breath is absolutely critical to controlling your volume. However, I've heard people trying to be louder really strain their voices. Often, clear articulation will make you sound louder and help the audience understand you. In fact, most of the time volume is not the problem. A lack of articulation is, just like the speaker in Las Vegas.

Timbre is a less-known term. The quality of your voice is

timbre. Do you have a smooth, lilting voice? Do you have a strident, strong voice? Timbre is the type of sound your voice makes, and most people aren't aware of this quality. Have you ever been in an airplane and heard one voice above all the white noise? That's an aggressive, strident timbre. Now think about the smooth, almost silky quality of a DJ on a jazz station. His timbre matches the quality of the music to create a pleasurable, consistent sound experience. You can alter your timbre depending on what you need to accomplish. I smooth out the sound of my voice if I want to soothe one of my children. Once I actually pulled out a growly, gravelly, mean voice when I felt threatened on a city street at night. I don't think that man expected that timbre from me, and he crossed back to the other side of the street.

Speed isacriticalaspectofbeingunderstoodandyoumayhaveto SLOW DOWN! Or try becoming comfortable with different speeds. At some point, if you speak too quickly, you'll be asked to slow down, but that can be really difficult. I speak quickly, so when I slow my speech intentionally, it feels like I'm fighting my way through molasses. However, it sounds just right to the audience. And remember, if you really want to make a point, you can combine several powerful tools to great effect: plant your body, raise your vocal volume, and speak very slowly to make a key point. Just channel Samuel L. Jackson.

Connection to breath is what gives us enough oxygen to speak. By breathing deeply before, during, and after a speech you'll have enough air to get through it and your body will be more relaxed. More on this when we break Rule #13.

Silence is your friend. Do not be afraid of it. Silence is as much a part of your voice as speaking is. Speakers chronically fill the slightest gap with *ummm* or *ahhhh*, or they increase their pace to fill the space. Unintentionally, this appears to your audience as nervousness. Silence allows your listeners to think about what you've said and allows you to create power in your speaking. Try using silence as a way to build drama or connect with your audience. Or use silence to take a break for yourself. Cross the stage, take a drink of water, refer to your notes. The silence that feels interminable to you feels like nothing to the audience.

That's a lot of stuff! But voice is part of your presenter tool kit. So sharpen it up a little. Experiment—do a few goofy exercises and see whether it works to bring out the baddest voice I just know you have.

YOU'LL HAVE TO USE A MICROPHONE SOMETIME

Okay, let's just admit it—microphones can be a pain. They can also magnify your badness, so best to figure them out.

If you are someone who thinks, "I can project my voice—forget the microphone," consider these stats:[14]

> Approximately 22 percent of American adults (36 million of us) report some degree of hearing loss.

> The National Institute on Deafness and Other Communication Disorders estimates that approximately 15 percent of Americans between the ages of twenty and sixty-nine (26 million people) have high-frequency hearing loss from exposure to loud sounds or noise.

> Only one out of five people who could benefit from a hearing aid actually wears one.

The point? If you have the option to use a mike, take it! Many people avoid using a microphone because it makes them feel uncomfortable. That is a terrible disservice to your audience.

Understand as well that people don't want to let on that they're having a problem. Your listeners may have hearing issues, but they will often suffer in silence rather than be singled out and embarrassed.

Becoming familiar with mikes is an important part of staying relaxed during your presentations. *Lavalieres* (or *lavs*) are a hands-free device. The microphone piece attaches to your lapel or even your head, giving you that Madonna vibe. Some are wireless, but most have a wire, so you must be able to attach the remote to your clothing, usually a waistband—it's not wise to wear a dress that has nowhere to attach your remote box. In fact, wires that are hidden in your jacket or blouse are less distracting to the audience.

Attach the lav so that it doesn't flap and create bumping sounds, and avoid long hair and clacking necklaces. Check your mike well in advance. A good mike will pick up your voice wherever it's positioned on your clothes. Avoid pulling it up to your mouth and uttering the annoying "Pfft, pfft—is this thing working?" in front of your audience. That's like screaming, "I'm an amateur."

Also remember that your microphone is on, and on you. Side comments will be heard by the entire audience. This gets pretty embarrassing if you forget your mike is attached and go to the bathroom. (If you think this doesn't happen very often, I know a conference center that hangs a sign in front of every toilet: Be Sure Your Microphone Is Off!)

Handheld microphones are the ultimate rock 'n roll front-man prop. Place the microphone in and out of its stand so that you can do it smoothly. Practice speaking with the microphone in your hand, like a prop, and also with it on a stand so that you can gesture. And then be sure to perfect the Rolling Stones spinning mike stand move. (Just kiddin'.) Hold a handheld microphone right up to your mouth. People who are unfamiliar with using a microphone hold it at their belt, which gives the audience a lovely amplification of the speaker's digestive tract.

Be sure to stay in control of the microphone, even when someone else is speaking. If you hand over a microphone to an audience member, you've handed over the presentation. What if this person has way too much to say? Stay in control of your microphone at all times. When an audience microphone is not in use, always repeat questions or comments. Even then, if you wonder at all about the clarity of a comment, repeat it to the audience before answering.

And for all microphones, learn the different setup options. Some facilities may have only portable speakers on stands. If you walk past the line of the speakers, your microphone will create the earsplitting squeal we all hate so much. Then the mike will stop working. If you plan to walk all around the room or go into the audience, check the range of your mike and the speakers in the room to be sure they can accommodate your plans—and be ready to improvise if you need to change.

For a short video on Voice,
visit www.ImprovEdge.com/videos

#8 and #9: Scan the back wall to simulate eye contact, and stand behind the podium

Scanning is fake, and podiums are really, really awful.

For some reason, the old rules use every trick possible to ... well, trick you. If something makes you uncomfortable, the rules immediately look for a workaround, some way to avoid the issue. So here's a shocker—attempting eye contact can make some people pretty nervous. Therefore, we have the awful Rule to Break #8, "Scan the back wall to simulate eye contact."

Over the last six years, I've been taking an informal poll. It's entirely anecdotal and has no official record. But in my classes, hundreds of people are subscribing to a really bad rule. At least 70 percent of the people I've asked verify that they've been told about a trick for eye contact, and it's this: If looking into the faces and eyes of the audience makes you nervous, just scan the back wall or look right over their heads, and no one will be able to tell the difference. The audience will think you're making eye contact with the row behind them.

What's the funniest part of this? When I ask people whether they think this technique works, they practically shout me down with "No!" They go on to tell me stories of watching someone use the technique and how fake it is. Even in a huge room with hundreds of audience members, they could always tell when someone was faking eye contact. It all goes back to making an authentic connection with the audience. An audience knows—can *feel*—that you don't really want to look at them and that you're skimming through without actually building a bridge to anyone.

So what's the answer? If you really do become nervous looking into the faces of other people when you present, I have several ideas I'd like to share with you.

> **Plant a friend**—There's nothing like a smiling, familiar face. Choose a friend you trust, who puts you at ease and won't make you more nervous. Have a friend you trust attend your presentation so that you know you have a safe haven in the sea of strangers. Just remember not to direct your entire presentation to them. Once you feel strong from their faithful glance, share some of that goodwill with another audience member. They might become your newest smiling friend.

> **Practice in conversation**—Become aware of times when you make eye contact in a casual, enjoyable conversation. It's easy with one person. How does it feel? What do you notice about your enjoyment, your connection to that person, to the interest they take in your comments? Now translate that into the next presentation you do for more than one person.

> **Make eye contact, and then take a break**—Give yourself small goals. Decide that you'll make eye contact for one full sentence with three people in a row. Then spend the next three to four sentences looking at the back wall, at your flip chart, or at your smiling friend. That break looking at a neutral place will allow you to breathe, calm your nerves, and then try it with a few more people. If you need a bit more time to gather yourself, walk over to the podium for a sip of water or to briefly consult your notes. That gives you

a chance to look away, keep breathing, and even be silent for a moment.

Uh-oh. Now I've done it. I've mentioned the podium. That takes us to the *really* bad Rule to Break #9, "Stand behind the podium." If you've come this far in the book, you already know how valuable your body is in making your presentations absolutely fabulous. So don't hide behind a podium.

A podium is just a big chunk of boring. It cuts off your ability to connect, influence, and engage with your audience. I've talked about how people are influenced by your body language. They more readily trust and connect with someone they can see in totality. And even if you are being authentic, a podium makes you a talking head. There's no getting around it. It anchors you, drags down your energy, and separates you from your audience.

If you need something to hold on to, use your notecards or the remote. Feel free to walk back and forth to a table when you need to refer to notes, sip water, or change a slide manually. And if the doggone podium has been planted right in the middle of the stage (you can imagine how I feel about that), ask if it can be moved to the side. Find out if it can be removed altogether. Worst case, lean against it and walk in front of it. Don't let the podium be the main event—you are!

**For a short video on Eye Contact,
click www.ImprovEdge.com/videos**

#10: Explain each topic

Tell stories! Stories are the most powerful way to share information.

Think about a favorite story from your childhood. It could be a fable, like *Goldilocks and the Three Bears*; a funny family story, like how your great-grandfather set the barn on fire; or a personal story, like your favorite vacation. I bet you can tell these stories without a hitch. When I ask a roomful of people to relate a fable, almost all of them can recall the characters, the conflict, and the moral. We also remember stories from TV shows, books, and movies.

Now, think about a PowerPoint presentation you saw about two months ago. How much of that information have you retained? Even if it was critical—and you promised yourself you'd remember—you probably asked for a copy of the slide deck because you knew you'd never be able to recall all the data. So how come *Goldilocks* is so clear, but data points aren't? Because Goldie has the advantage of being embedded in a story. Neuroscience is constantly asking why our brains retain some things and trash others. We are only beginning to understand why stories are such an effective presentation and leadership technique.

Our understanding of the power of stories began through research in the field of artificial intelligence. For a long time, we believed memory was like a filing cabinet, where events and impressions were neatly organized according to a hierarchy. In trying to emulate the complexity of the human brain, however, researchers began to uncover the fact that our memory is stored based on *context*, not content.[15] Have you ever smelled something that takes you suddenly back with alarming clarity to a moment you haven't thought of in years? Or have you ever returned to a place only to be flooded with memories of the time you spent there? That's because the context of those memories was activated and you could retrieve them.

Neuroscientists have also learned that depending on how you choose to communicate, you can activate different areas of your listeners' brains. When you use only data, you activate the language-processing parts of the brain. So, all the brain is doing is decoding the words. Simple... and boring.

However, if you use descriptive, compelling words tied to a story, a surprise, or a metaphor, your brain and the brains of your listeners begin to function in a whole new way. If you say "the dog's bristle-brush fur" or "the cold, slimy rock," the sensory receptors in the brain light up. If you say words related to smell, like "cinnamon" or "coffee," the olfactory sensors start working. If you talk about "gripping the wheel with all my might" or "running so fast my legs pumped to my heartbeat," the motion portions of the brain are activated.[16] Cool, right?

As a matter of fact, Uri Hasson of Princeton University has found that you can plant emotions and thoughts into your listeners' brains through storytelling.[17] That's why it's so common for people to believe a story is theirs when they've actually heard it elsewhere. The power of the story in their own brains is so immediate, it feels as though they experienced the events themselves. That's also why we cry when we hear someone else's sad story or become happy or enraged when we hear about the triumphs or indignities of others. It's also why our parents' or siblings' versions of stories become ours as well. We may have been too young to really remember an event, but the story told to us by family members plants itself and feels as though it's ours.

Let's face it, our brains love and respond to stories. And if you're striving to be the baddest presenter you can be, it's time to start experimenting with storytelling. If you feel too self-conscious to use your own tales, borrow stories from experts, the news, and fables to bring your ideas to life.

Storytelling and context are powerful. A woman in one of our workshops used a narrative device—analogy—particularly well. In trying to help people understand a charity she worked for, she described it as "Pony Express meets the underground railroad." She was a driver for last-minute rescues of abandoned pets from "high-kill" animal pounds. Although many families want to adopt those highly vulnerable pets, they cannot afford or cannot take time off work to drive many states away to pick them up. The organization has a network of drivers who pass off the just-saved animals from one car to another, across state lines, until they make it to their new homes. As she told her story, we had the drama of galloping horses and hidden tunnels in our heads. Those elements made her presentation rich and engaging—and I remember it.

Stories create a sense of culture and belonging. When a child asks her parents why so many generations of their family have been firefighters, the parents pass down the story of great-grandpa setting the barn on fire. Even though you may not have been alive, it makes everyone laugh anyway. Then the parents relate how great-grandpa swore to fight fires from then on and became the first firefighter in the family.

Organizations also use stories to create a culture and communicate who they are, just like a family. Companies often talk about their hardworking, humble, or unexpected beginnings. Colonel Sanders started Kentucky Fried Chicken cooking in a white suit so that the flour wouldn't show on dark fabric. Post-It notes were perceived as a huge flop and shelved for years. Then one of 3M's researchers began using them to mark his hymnal and noticed that they didn't damage the pages. Steve Jobs started Apple out of his garage. Employees in a big successful company will feel the same pride as the founder if they look around at their huge offices and realize that it all began in a garage.

Stories, as researchers know, create connection and context. You've heard me raving about how speakers transform when they connect to a passionate story and share it with other people. So can you transform the mundane to the meaningful. This is where all the rule-breaking and advice come together to change the way we engage our audiences.

And here's where I want you to start thinking about stories in a much larger sense. So be warned: we're about to enter the most controversial section of this book. We're ready to tackle the subject of data and how to present it.

For a short video on Storytelling, click www.ImprovEdge.com/videos

#11: Have all your bullets on PowerPoint slides

Bullets are so called because they kill good presentations. PowerPoint numbs the brain. *You* are the presentation!

PowerPoint is a scourge—on our ability to communicate effectively and keep an audience awake. Worse yet, it has become a substitute for us. When I ask people in my classes how they begin to prepare for a presentation, almost everyone says they sit down at a computer and start working on slides. What? Figuring out your purpose, action, audience, bookends... everything should come before you open PowerPoint. And when you finally get around to considering visual aids, always ask yourself—do I really need PowerPoint slides at all?

Most PowerPoint decks just stink. They are loaded with data in small type, go on forever, and are filled with animations of swooshing words. Not to mention that the data is often so riveting that the audience should be provided with toothpicks to prop open their eyes. Over the last decade, I've worked with professionals from the C-level down, and 99 percent of them use PowerPoint miserably.

It's like the costume wearing the character. Have you ever seen a kid wearing a thoroughly impressive scary costume? Although they're shy, hiding behind their mom and barely speaking, they think that their costume makes them scary. It's the same with PowerPoint—we believe that the slides are the presentation, not us. PowerPoint is a lot like email: it's a perfectly good tool that should make our lives easier, but it's become a time-sucking, efficiency-mauling monster.

Everything has a story behind it. The shame is that so often we choose to present data and information in the most boring way possible. We fail to connect all that information to a story. And it's time to realize that data and information always tell a story. The point is what is it? Are you willing to tell it?

The format of PowerPoint—"bulletizing" and simplifying ideas—has taken over the substance of what we are trying to say. Edward Tufte (the rock star of charts and graphs) says that PowerPoint is a competent slide manager, but instead of supplementing a presentation, it has become a substitute for one. Tufte also points out how a PowerPoint presentation that should have been a technical report helped lead to the *Columbia* space shuttle disaster.[18] As Beth Dickey reported in her article on safety assessments at NASA, "The biggest lesson, Roe [leader of the NASA Engineering and Safety Center] said, is to curb the practice of 'PowerPoint engineering.'" The Columbia report chided NASA engineers for their reliance on bulleted presentations. In four studies, inspectors came to agree that PowerPoint slides are not a good tool for providing substantive documentation of results. "We think it's important to go back to the basics," Roe said. "We're making it a point with the agency that engineering organizations need to go back to writing engineering reports." Some in the Department of Defense consider PowerPoint to be dangerous because it can create the illusion of understanding and the illusion of control. Some problems in the world are not bulletizable.[19]

Years ago, my company partnered with a great branding agency. A large financial client had hired them to create a PowerPoint deck for a critical meeting with clients and employees. It was a really big deal, and the finance company handed over creation of the slides to the agency because it wanted the deck to be perfect. Again, everyone was focusing on the PowerPoint file as the central delivery system. And, you guessed it, no one practiced with it in advance. No one at the agency ever looked at it other than on the computer screen, and no one at the financial firm ever put it up on a screen until the VP was standing on stage. Turns out the designers used type and pictures that were too small. It was so bad, even the VP giving the presentation had to squint from her position on the stage. It was an embarrassing, unprofessional combination of lack of practice and using the wrong medium. In other words, a hot mess.

When you want to make the greatest impact, first try using devices such as storytelling, music, or pictures. Then, only if you really need it, should you consider PowerPoint. Surprises, expertise, and good ideas have far more impact than another predictable presentation.

A slide full of data is a distraction and often does the exact opposite of what we intend—it undermines our credibility. As soon as you throw up a slide with lots of information, people start reading the slide and stop listening to you. The point of standing up in front of an audience is to let them know that you are the expert. You know your material, and you are the one telling the story. If your technology should fail, you can still present without the visual cues.

Why do all those numbers need to be up there? I know—you will shout and scream and insist that people want to see the data. So why can't all those numbers be in a handout to pass out later? Or drop the information into the speaker notes in PowerPoint. When your presentation is over, you can send out the notes so that everyone has the slides with all the data.

NUMBERS AND STATISTICS CAN TELL A STORY

If you do your homework, figure out the story you want to tell, and infuse your passion and purpose into a presentation, the data can be incredible. Think about this. Suppose you ditch the slide with eighty numbers on it that no one past the second row can see. Instead, show the bell curve it signifies. Then you quote the applicable numbers and tell the story of why this information matters. Does it show an uptick in performance because of the new sales system? Does it hint at a trend that could change the way you do business? Do you have an opinion about the data? If you stand tall, tell the story of the data yourself, and promise them the numbers later, guess what they'll remember? That you are an expert. That you know your stuff. That you're the one they want to hear from again.

If you stand around referring to the slide constantly, guess who's the expert. The slide.

A VP from a major fast-food chain made a real breakthrough in our class once. His first presentation was about raising the price of their hamburgers by twenty-five cents. He talked about the inevitable profit but also the strain on customers who did not have a high income and relied on this restaurant chain for meals fairly often. It was a lot of general information buried in ratios. I asked him if he had a personal example of someone—could he tell a story to help us understand why he opposed the price increase? His next version was incredible. He got rid of the ratios and instead used very understandable numbers—a real person's budget. And that real person, Max, was a manager at one of their own stores. The VP took Max's total salary, showed his daily and monthly expenses, and guess what? A twenty-five cent price increase would have made it impossible for Max to afford lunch at his own place of work each day. We were floored. It was a convincing, passionate story about the importance of keeping the hamburger price low. And he did it with three simple support slides.

It's time to think about ways to simplify your slides and stop making them the center of attention. So let's walk through some simple suggestions to get there—to put the slide in its place as the backdrop, and get you in the spotlight.

10/24. This ratio means that you should try not to have more than ten words per slide, never smaller than 24-point type. Okay, start shouting. I've heard plenty of bellyaching about this concept: "I have important data to cover! My boss expects me to show her all the numbers! This is how we've always done it here!" Yes, you're right. Your data is very important. But tiny type numbs the brain, and the correct place for data is in a handout. Your slides should be clean and simple—and a backdrop for *you*. And don't try to cheat. A number counts as one of your ten words. I promise that I have never seen a slide that couldn't be broken down into 10/24. And it's better to have ten slides that follow the 10/24 ratio than one slide that's a mess.

Please don't read your slides. Most of your audience has completed the third grade. They can read. So give them something new—add engaging stories, tell them the outcome of the study, remind them why this information is important and who or what it may affect. Your part of the speech should not be on the slide. We don't want to see the script; we want to see the performance.

Use pictures to illustrate points. One of the best slides I've ever seen was simply a photo of a pile of sawdust, with more sawdust falling from above to increase the pile. I was at my publisher's retreat, and a great book marketer was discussing a rather complicated concept about author output. He was addressing the huge stress we all felt to create so much content, every day, for multiple channels. However, by using the concept of sawdust, he reminded us that every author has lots of content that is shaved away, edited out, or isn't used. That "sawdust"—content left over from our big works of writing—could probably provide months of supply. He used no bullet points or statistics, yet I can clearly recall the concept, his five or six points, and his recommendations. All because his analogy and image were so striking. Pictures really are worth a thousand words.

And one more thing—leave the lights up. It's more important that the audience see your face than every detail of your slides. Besides, you don't want to give them an invitation to nap.

SPEAKING OF TECHNOLOGY— WHAT ABOUT VIDEOCONFERENCES?

Just like PowerPoint and email, videoconferencing is a technology that should save us all a lot of money and time. It allows geographically dispersed teams to see each other, it allows leaders to be known more personally, and it helps us feel connected. It's also making people really uncomfortable, and we're not sure how to use it. Actors know that there's a big difference between performing on stage and performing for the camera. Everything has to be bigger on stage and live in person. The camera, on the other hand, magnifies us, so less is always more. Here are a few tips for managing videoconference presentations.

Remember that all the content and format suggestions still apply. Having a purpose, action, passion, and bookends and engaging in lots of practice can only help you improve your persona on camera as a video presenter. Practice is especially critical so that you can become comfortable with being on camera and focusing on the audience.

Make eye contact. We're always tempted to look at ourselves (usually in a little box in the corner) rather than at the person on the screen. That little box is much like a mirror—distracting. Practice looking right at the person or people with whom you are videoconferencing. You'll soon be able to feel the connection of eye contact and focus on that other person.

Environment still matters. If you can create a clean background, it will lessen distractions for the viewer. Having lots of stuff behind you—or, if you are home, seeing a pet or child walk across the background—drags focus from your presentation. Can you hang a curtain or move your computer so that there's a plain wall behind you?

Be patient and have a backup plan. Technology such as videoconferencing still has lots of glitches. When the connection doesn't go as planned, be patient and keep trying. If you let frustration creep into your face or voice, it will affect your audience. It's also a great idea to have another form of videoconferencing available if one service should tank. And let your audience know that you have a plan. "If the connection fails, I'll call you back. If for some reason we can't reconnect on this service, text me and we'll go to service B."

Allow time to feel confident. Be sure you have on a nice shirt, have a moment to brush your hair, and that lunch isn't stuck in your teeth. Do a few breathing exercises and dial in early so that you don't feel rushed.

Be creative. If you can share small visual aids but still keep your personality on camera, it's a great combination. I once watched a presenter use little postcards and props to illustrate her points instead of turning off the camera and going to a slide presentation. It was really fun to still see her face and still get all the information—it was like a minimized flip chart.

Here at my company, we even engage in improvisation via videoconference. We've had facilitators across multiple time zones use phone lines, videoconference, social media, and live exercises all at once. Did it always go flawlessly? No. Was it fun, challenging, and effective? Yes. And one of the most surprising outcomes of our insistence on pushing the boundaries of our presentations was newfound courage for our clients. They've said that before our workshops, they never used their technology. Now that they've "played" with it, virtual meetings and presentations happen all the time. So go ahead—get ready for your close-up and have fun.

COURAGEOUSLY BAD

At an international media and sports conglomerate, my ensemble worked with an executive who bowled us over with the power of her PowerPoint. This vice president (I'll call her Ellie) was a funny, intelligent, likeable finance professional. But during her first formal presentation on company investments, Ellie disappeared. It was as though someone had stolen her personality and replaced her with a serious, low-energy shell of herself. And that shell was pasted to her PowerPoint. The slides were complicated, each was full of data points, and she looked back at the screen throughout the presentation.

I realized that Ellie was suffering from two different issues. First, she believed that because her subject was finance, she wasn't allowed to interject any levity. Second, she was grappling with how to present herself as an executive and felt she needed to come across as more serious.

Important information doesn't necessarily have to be presented in a serious manner. As a matter of fact, the numbers Ellie was showing had to do with her company's success and its plans for the future. It was exciting stuff, and once Ellie sat down, the stories behind those numbers began to pour out of her. She even laughed out loud recounting how a project had come off so well for her department. We urged her to find ways to show the important data in an uplifting way. I saw Ellie's eyes light up, and she said she would surprise us the next day with her edits.

In discussing Ellie's second issue, her classmates wondered why she, who was an expert in her field, "hid" behind the numbers on the screen and didn't show her warm personality. She shared that it was sometimes difficult to be a woman in her field, a combination of finance and sports. She wanted to be sure she was not discounted because of her age and gender. She was hesitant to be too opinionated, so she let the slides speak for her. She also peeled away behaviors that might be seen as frivolous. Psychologists have long known that gender can affect how comfortable people feel in showing power, and Ellie was carefully considering that balance and how it might affect her career.[20] But Ellie loved her work. Inside, she was really dying to express those feelings.

The comments from her colleagues seemed to ignite an ah-ha moment for Ellie. She dove into the exercises on expressing passion, driving purpose, and using hooks and closings.

The next morning, when Ellie presented again, we were amazed. She removed all the extraneous data from her slides and used photos, graphs, stories, and analogies. She even got the entire audience to do the wave, just like you see in sports stadiums. She still delivered all the important information, but she did it in a way that spotlighted her as a funny, energetic, incredibly smart expert. The slides became a backdrop, and her presentation was incredible. All the data was provided afterward in a handout, and she expressed her opinions and suggestions in a straightforward, balanced way. It was pure Ellie, and completely effective.

I've seen only a few people courageous enough to totally reassess the use of PowerPoint and visual aids. By reconfiguring slides as Ellie did, you can actually communicate a stronger message. Or, by completely getting rid of PowerPoint, you might just elevate your presentation and yourself. I remember an aviation engineer who ditched his slides and had us all create paper airplanes together. We came to deeply understand his concepts and connected to his ideas in a way we couldn't when they were just numbers on a slide.

I challenge you to be courageous. Slim down your data, use pictures, or get rid of PowerPoint altogether. And watch your audience wake up.

**For a short video on Visual Aids,
click www.ImprovEdge.com/videos**

THREE

OOPS!

Staying Bad, No Matter What Happens

There's a great concept in improvisation. It's called "Oops to Eureka!" On the improv stage—heck, on any stage—things go wrong sometimes. Or they change, not in a worrisome way, but an unexpected way. "Oops" is the response when we realize something unexpected has happened. The key is to make those instances become "Eurekas" rather than disasters. This might require quite a change in mindset for many people. It's hard not to minimize or walk away from our Oops moments. In improv, we're not allowed to ignore the unexpected. We're obligated to acknowledge it and keep it in the show. In reality, the unexpected is improv's stock in trade. Even within our own troupes, we're constantly trying to surprise each other with unexpected suggestions and scenes.

Scientists do the same thing: they never assume to know the outcome; they embrace "mistakes" or the unexpected as fully as they do the predictable. The questions become "What wonderful thing will happen now that the agenda has flown out the window?" "What discovery will be made?"

This endless positivity is also rooted in an improv concept—"Yes, and...." The reason that improvisers can arrive onstage without a script, props, or costumes and create an entire play out of thin air is because we've all agreed to say "Yes, and...." No matter what crazy thing occurs, we agree to validate it and then build on it. For example, if your partner points his finger at you and says,

"Hands up! I've got a gun," you don't say, "That's not a gun, that's your finger." You put your hands up and say, "Yes, that's a gun. And it's the one I bought you for our anniversary! How romantic, darling." And we're off to the races.

Validating the unexpected in just this way is crucial to managing issues in your presentations. Yes, unexpected things will happen. Sometimes they'll be awful, such as when the technology you're using crashes. Your Eureka might be finding out just how well you manage on your feet or discovering that using the flip chart instead of the PowerPoint slides engages the audience more. Sometimes these surprises will be wonderful and make you feel like a million bucks—for example, a person raising his hand to tell you and the whole audience how valuable your presentation is and that he'll use your advice right away. In that case, your Eureka might be to realize that your presentation should become an article or a blog that you can share with more people.

Gene Perrett was Bob Hope's lead comedy writer and also won three Emmys writing for *The Carol Burnett Show*. After years in live show business, he once wrote, "All of the complications you encounter onstage are... fixable. Remember that you are the featured act in this performance; the problem is a bit player. It will make its entrance and its exit, but you will remain as the star. Never let your audience forget that."[1]

This final section is dedicated to debunking all the rules out there about the things you don't plan for. You no longer have to be a victim of the unexpected—you can embrace it.

#12: If something goes wrong, act like nothing happened

Everyone knows what happened, and ignoring it is weird. Acknowledge it, deal with it, move on.

Let's just dive in and look at a really tough situation I once encountered.

I facilitated a training about diversity and inclusion for experienced new hires at a top professional-services firm. In a group of smart, capable, and highly diverse new associates, a white male began to attack the content. He said that all this training was useless and that he felt it was "stupid" to be so careful and correct. And didn't I agree that this was all show? It was so shocking and embarrassing, I looked around expecting to see the *Candid Camera* guys. I'm not kidding. It was like I was trapped in a really bad movie. He recounted all the other companies he'd worked for that made a big show of diversity and inclusion but never supported them. I get the frustration, but ding ding! Attacking your new company's training on your first day at work may be a career-limiting move. Not to mention that this guy had actually landed in a place that took diversity *very* seriously and put their money where their mouth was.

In Chinese, the word for "crisis" is the same word for "opportunity."

—*Fortune cookie*

I took a moment to pull myself together. I looked him in the eye and nodded and breathed. Then I started, "Yes, you seem very frustrated." By my acknowledging his state of mind, he agreed, and I said, "And I understand how your past experience may make this a difficult topic, and I appreciate your honesty. Would you be willing to stick with us today, hear our stance on this topic, and then you and I and some of the leaders can discuss your concerns afterward?" He agreed to this, and I was able to move on. Yeesh!

The in-house trainer, who had been watching, was a little freaked out when I spoke with her at the break. "That was great," she said. "I would have been so afraid to say anything to him—he was so inappropriate! I think I would have ignored him and just gone on to the next section."

You've got to have a few tools in your kit to deal with the unexpected. The key here was honestly accepting what's going on in the room. So many times, presentation primers encourage us to ignore embarrassing things, but the truth is that ignoring them just creates the proverbial "elephant in the room." When something happens that goes unacknowledged, no one can concentrate. All they're thinking about is the elephant—that big, bulky creature that everyone knows is in the room but no one will talk about.

So what do you do when something unexpected happens? *Acknowledge it, deal with it, move on.*

Those are the three magic moves. If something happens, you've got to take control and be clear that you know what's going on. I acknowledged the incident I described by affirming the speaker's frustration. I dealt with it by taking responsibility not only for his issues but also for the audience. The goal was to get back to the content instead of falling into an uncomfortable or emotional conversation. That was tabled for later, with experts from the firm I could lean on. Once that was done, I didn't revisit it or refer to it again. These concepts—acknowledge it, deal with it, and move on—will serve you well. Let me give you both a good and a bad example.

I attended a luncheon program about intellectual property. A young attorney was our presenter, and he had an impressive amount of experience in intellectual property law. Unfortunately, he thought that the venue would have a screen and projector, and he'd prepared a PowerPoint document to go with his speech. When he mounted the stage to present, he introduced himself and apologized, mentioning that he had prepared some slides, would send the document to anyone who gave him a card, and would present without it. That should have been the last mention of the PowerPoint. We, as the audience, couldn't see it and didn't care about it.

But then this young attorney proceeded to refer to the PowerPoint that wasn't there (and its graphs) seventeen times in the course of a thirty-minute presentation. The irony is he didn't need it. He knew all his information, was an obvious expert in the area, and was quite a charismatic speaker. Unfortunately, he kept drawing our attention away from his brilliance by reminding us that his carefully prepared PowerPoint was not in attendance. What a shame! He acknowledged the issue and dealt with it by giving a speech full of good information, but he could not move on.

Conversely, here's a great example of really using the *acknowledge it, deal with it, move on* approach. A major state university held a ceremony for a sports star to name a scholarship in his honor. In attendance were the sports star, the president of the university, and the governor of the state. The sports star came up on stage first, and about thirty seconds into his talk, construction noises began in the hallway right off the atrium. And I'm not talking just hammers. There was loud banging, weird screeches, and growling power tools. Worse yet, it was intermittent. It would stop, and just as we'd all think it was over, it would start up again, only louder. The sports star ignored the disruption, persevered, and finally concluded his speech.

Next up to the stage came the president of the university. He too chose to ignore the incredibly obtrusive noises. (Whenever I tell this story in a class, I do it while banging on tables and crashing over flip charts to give a sense of the auditory pandemonium.) It was so distracting! No one could concentrate on the speeches.

Finally, the governor of the state mounted the dais. He paused, looked meaningfully at the hallway, turned to the sports star and said, "I knew you were planning to build a shrine to yourself, but this is ridiculous!" The entire audience cracked up in laughter and relief. He had at last acknowledged the event, and not only did he acknowledge the awful distraction, he made a joke of it. Then he dealt with it this way: "Folks, there's some work going on next door, but the important thing is that our university is growing. And we're here today to honor an amazing man." By letting the audience know that there was no stopping the noise, and that priorities were straight, everyone could focus on the event at hand. It was as though the noises vanished. He then moved on —"Let's talk about this great person!"—and gave his full speech without ever mentioning the commotion again.

I presented at a women's conference in Dallas for about four hundred attendees. One of the principles I talked about that day was "Oops to Eureka!" Wow, did I ever have to live my philosophy that day.

I arrived at the venue an hour in advance, as is my ritual, to check all the technology, see the layout, and greet attendees.

Everything looked perfect. When my keynote began, everything worked fine. Then my slides went crazy. They were blank, had gibberish instead of words, or were a wash of weird colors. I let the audience know there was an issue, pulled out a backup memory stick I always carry with the presentation, and called on the tech team to go to the laptop and work on it. While they worked on the visuals, I told the audience that I would continue with my speech.

I got through another five minutes (which felt like fifty to me), but the crew was obviously having no luck, and they were more distracting than helpful. Finally, I said, "Who needs slides? Shall we continue without the slides and give this great tech team a break?" The whole audience applauded, and the tech team sat down. It was a perfect example of "Oops to Eureka!," and I used it as a model to inspire my audience.

Dealing with unexpected events can have all sorts of incarnations. When something really goes wrong, you might need to pause to deal with it. That's okay. The audience appreciates your control. Then move on, and don't look back.

On the subject of slalom waterskiing:
"If you don't fall every now and then,
you're not working hard enough."

—David A. Hough, my father

For a short video on Managing the Unexpected,
visit www.ImprovEdge.com/videos

#13: Ignore your nerves, and they will go away

Only zombies never get nervous. Nerves are good— breathe and embrace them.

Everybody gets nervous at some point. If you feel ill and nervous, have an upset stomach, a dry mouth, or shaking hands, you may feel at the mercy of these terrible stress reactions.

The truth is, nerves are a great bad thing! They are the body's way of telling you that you care, that this is important. Adrenaline kicks in, energy flows through you, and your body is ready for anything. The key is to think of your reactions as good—to recognize them when they appear and use the excess energy. For example, when I'm nervous, my neck gets hot and turns a little red. Rather than sensing that heat and getting worried, I've trained myself to think, "Oh, there goes my neck again. It's about three minutes before I go on, so this is good. I'm going to take that extra energy and force it out through my smile." An awareness like that allows you to draw something from your nerves rather than be enslaved by them. Frame it this way: "I understand that I'll always have butterflies in my stomach. Now I can help them fly in formation."

In a recent class, I worked with a woman, Ava, who suffered from the worst physical nerves I'd ever seen. Even from the back of the room, you could see her entire body physically shaking. Her face turned red, and sweat ran down her scalp, neck, arms, and back. I worried she'd become lightheaded and possibly pass out if we didn't deal with the issue.

The irony was that Ava was a great presenter. She was humorous, used funny examples from her experience, and really exuded her authentic personality. Her physical reactions, however, were sending her into tailspins of anxiety, and she had the perception that she was an awful presenter, which simply was not true.

Ava also had a bad habit of giving a "tell" near the end of her presentation. A "tell" is a poker term. It's often a subconscious or involuntary physical movement or look in the eyes that lets the other players at the table figure out whether your hand is good or bad.

Ava's tells were explicit. Just as she stepped off the stage, she'd roll her eyes and heave a sigh. Or, right in the middle of a perfect section, she'd drop her shoulders and say, "I'm so nervous I can't hardly make it through!" She was hoping for the audience to feel some sympathy for her. But remember what you already learned about audiences? They are sympathetic and forgiving. An audience might have noticed Ava shaking but been impressed that she did so well despite her nerves. Or if audience members saw the perspiration, they might have thought, "Gee, must be hot on stage." However, there was no reason for Ava to trash herself through physical or verbal tells.

Ava learned a couple of key skills for dealing with nerves:

› **Breath and breathing techniques**—Having plenty of oxygen is critical to managing the nervous system. When Ava used careful, measured breathing techniques before, during, and after her presentation, her shaking reduced by half. (More on this in the next section.)

> **Power statement**—Remember how your body can teach
> you confidence? In addition to having Ava breathe, I told
> her to repeat to herself, "I'm a great presenter. My nervous-
> ness is energy I use to be great! When I shake, I know I
> care, and that makes me a great presenter." Powerful "I am"
> statements always raise your confidence. Rather than think-
> ing about the future—"I will be"—you have to put what you
> want into the right now.

The idea of a power statement is rooted in the concept
of current reality—and a beautiful example called "A Letters."
Rosamund Stone Zander and Benjamin Zander explored the
behavioral transformations that occur in high-level music students when they embrace the reality of receiving an A grade at
the beginning of their semester. Normally, students scratch and
claw all semester to achieve an A at the end. The students write a
letter at the beginning of the semester explaining to their professor why they received an A. Those letters reveal everything each
student really needs to master his or her goals. It also gives them
an inspiring vision of success. In their minds, they have already
attained the summit and can now move forward with confidence
and excitement rather than fear.[2]

Once Ava began breathing and using "I am" statements, she
felt completely different about the stage. Even though she still
shook and perspired a bit, her breathing allowed her to feel in
control. The power statement also encouraged her body and
brain to drop the tells—she didn't feel the need to apologize and
berate herself. That grounding will affect an audience as well—
people might notice the shaking, but as long as Ava is her passionate self, no one cares.

BREATH IS YOUR SECRET WEAPON

Most people ignore breathing. They feel too silly or self-conscious to engage in breathing techniques that will help them. If you think deep breathing and relaxation techniques are only for yoga pros, well, you're flat out wrong. Understanding your breath and how it can support your presentation and presence is a key underpinning of power. How do you think actors sound so commanding and dancers look as though the most demanding sequence is a snap? It's because part of their mastery is breathing and using that oxygen to fuel their performances.

When people get nervous, they start to breathe in a quick, shallow way that only reaches their neck. Then they sound weak, look terrified, and can't manage their shaking hands. As a matter of fact, I once watched a major executive pass out on stage—the dude fell like a tree. He did just what your sixth-grade choir instructor warned you not to do—he locked his knees and forgot to breathe!

Whenever you encounter an unusual situation, your body reacts. You may feel all sorts of physical responses to the fear and uncertainty of situations such as interviews, presentations, and unexpected moments when you're put on the spot. A racing heart, dry mouth, blanking, shaking or clammy hands—these are all ways that your body responds to the sudden flood of chemicals to your brain. Your body is reacting to a primal influx of cortisol and other stress chemicals that urges you to fight or flee the unknown. And since running away isn't really a good solution to modern-day stress, let's explore some techniques to manage it.

The number one, most important technique to manage nerves is breathing. One of the first things we lose in stressful situations is oxygen. The tricky part is that we don't recognize the loss — we begin to breathe rapidly and shallowly, we hold our breath involuntarily, and suddenly we're close to passing out. Starting to breathe deeply well before you step into an uncomfortable situation is absolutely essential. Find your own breathing technique that can calm your physical reactions and get accustomed to using it. Even seasoned presenters, salespeople, and executives know that when they manage their breathing, they feel calmer and can cope better.

Dr. Andrew Weil suggests an excellent breathing technique based on a specific ratio: 4:7:8. Breathe in through your nose to a count of four. Hold that breath for a count of seven. Release the breath through your mouth with a whooshing noise to a count of eight. By focusing and repeating this exercise, you actually trick your nervous system into calming down.[3]

I've used this technique many times to calm myself in the car on my way to an important meeting. I've used it right before stepping on stage. I even used it once when I left an argument. In each of those situations, my mind was racing and my body was reacting. By bringing oxygen into my body and giving my brain a calming ratio to focus on, I became myself and calmed down enough to think and deal. People often recommend counting to ten before you say something you might regret, but I would suggest breathing to ten.

After thousands of presentations, shows, performances, and workshops in my various careers, I'm so happy when the butterflies show up before each one. It's confirmation that I still care—that no matter who the audience is, my body is getting nervous and my adrenaline is pumping in anticipation. The day I don't get a bit anxious is the day I pick a new career.

**For a short video on Channeling Your Nerves,
visit www.ImprovEdge.com/videos**

#14: Control your emotions at all times

Passion and emotion are okay.

So let's discuss the dark side of passion. Have you ever been in a conversation with someone who made you feel uncomfortable? Maybe they shared more about themselves than you cared to know. Or perhaps they showed emotion that felt overwrought, offensive, or unnecessary to you. That's a real fear for many presenters. They don't want to be *that* person. But their fear may be keeping them from connecting with their audience in a meaningful and authentic way.

Emotional intelligence is a key concept in managing yourself as a presenter. It refers to the ability of people to step back and understand what emotions are driving and affecting both themselves and others. Part of being emotionally aware, and eventually being able to influence others (your primary objective in making a presentation), is having an awareness of self. And, if you don't know yourself, you can't know others and meet their needs. Self-awareness involves recognizing a feeling as it happens and remaining neutral about it rather than getting carried away with it; it's being fully aware of your mood and thoughts about your mood. When this is the case, you're better able to control and choose your behaviors. Without it, you're blind to emotions and might end up doing things or being someone you don't want to.

Daniel Goleman, the primary researcher in the field of

emotional intelligence, identifies a second component of being emotionally aware as *self-regulation*.[4] We have little control over when we are going to be swept away by an emotion or what the emotion will be, but we do have a say in how long it lasts. The emotional brain can overpower, even paralyze, the thinking brain —as when a presenter blanks on stage. When emotions over- whelm concentration, our working memory is swamped. We can no longer hold in our mind all the information relevant to the task at hand; we can't "think straight." That's dangerous ter- ritory when you are on stage. The goal is to regulate our feelings and manage them so that they are beneficial and not harmful.

Matt Jauchius is the executive vice president and chief mar- keting officer for Nationwide Insurance. Nationwide is one of the largest insurance and financial services companies in the world. Matt has a big presence and is clearly comfortable and capable as a presenter. He is especially effective because he remains authen- tic—if he makes a mistake or is surprised, he takes it in stride, which makes him all the more approachable and human.

Matt's in front of customers, the media, and stakeholders every day. That's enough to make even the coolest cucumber sweat. And he admits that at times, an emotion or passion can really take you by surprise. He told me he learned one of his secrets in dealing with stress, anger, sadness, or frustration years ago from a mentor. He said, "I'll never forget—he told me to strive to be more clinical. Let me repeat; strive to be more clini- cal. When you feel emotion taking over, and you're about to say, email, or do something you might regret, become a scientist." In effect, he was encouraged to take a step back, examine the sit- uation as if it were an experiment, and observe. Breathe, look around, and think about all the angles. As a presenter, if you find yourself in a combative, stressful, or difficult situation, strive to be more clinical. You have every right to pause, breathe, reconsider, ask an open-ended question to get the other person talking, or change course.

Having said this, I don't mean to indicate that you should be emotionless during a presentation. Remember, passion and authenticity are at the core of being your baddest you. But it's also wise to learn how to manage yourself.

You might want to set boundaries for yourself that are comfortable, that you consider in advance when you are calm. Just remember: emotion happens. It can move us, and yes, sometimes, you may lose a little control or manage less than perfectly. That's okay. You'll learn a lot about yourself in the process, and honest feedback from your listeners will only help you as well.

Now, here are some stories about excessive passion for you to consider as you decide how emotion works for you.

JUAN, THE PRIVATE PERSON

Juan was an executive for a global media company. He had a very cool career—he managed the finances for TV shows and movies. He lived and worked in LA and was on the set quite often during filming. We asked him to give a presentation about something that filled him with passion.

I thought he'd talk about some fabulous work in the movies. But he actually shared a simple and fun story about family movie night. He had two young daughters at the time, and every Friday night, he, his wife, and their kids would share popcorn as they snuggled on the couch to watch G-rated princess movies. After long weeks, often filled with travel and multimillion-dollar negotiations, he so looked forward to it. It was a great presentation, and the whole class saw a relaxed, smiling version of a guy who was usually quite serious.

What surprised us all was his discussion afterward. He said that in the totality of his career, he had never shared anything so private at work. The story seemed very straightforward, simple, and nothing out of the ordinary. But to Juan, it was monumental. He strove to be a completely professional person for work and never shared aspects of his family life. Telling that story was hard for him. But he admitted that it felt good to make a connection with his colleagues in the room.

After considerable discussion, Juan began to realize how important sharing bits of himself could be, not just for effective presentations, but for good leadership. His team would probably love to know about his family and his simple Friday tradition. A little bit of vulnerability can go a long way. We also talked about defining parameters in his mind. He wanted to share more, and he'd be able to do that effectively if he clarified in advance what he felt comfortable sharing. This lesson was profound for him.

TOM, THE OVERSHARER

We work with a large insurance firm every year in its emerging-leader program. Tom was an energetic participant who had no trouble getting up in front of people. He was straightforward and engaged with everyone.

He told the class honestly that one of his biggest coaching points at work was that he shared too much personal information with people. He'd been coached that it made people feel uncomfortable—they never knew what to do with the information or didn't understand why he had told them. It frustrated him. He revealed what he did because he believed in bringing his whole self to work. He wanted people to know him so that he could truly be himself. This is a great attitude and showed a really honest, open nature.

The other detail to consider, however, is environment. There are many environments where openness, full disclosure, and honesty are embraced and valued. Tom happened to work in a more conservative industry, with somewhat formal standards of conduct. His style simply wasn't working in that setting. And even in very open environments, it's important to be sensitive to others' preferences.

During his passion presentation, Tom talked about being a father. True to form, he shared the fact that he was an absent father for his first son, and that his son, sadly, had been incarcerated. It was the wake-up call of his life and changed how he dealt with all his kids.

I made him break down his presentation decisions for us. His action was to inform people about a difficult part of his life, and his purpose was for the group to know him better. A few of his classmates told him that if they'd had that conversation at work, they would have been flummoxed—and extremely uncomfortable. Some people felt okay about it, but many said it would make them avoid him in the future.

The answer to Tom's problem lay in clarifying his purpose and action. As I've said, the action "to inform" is weak, as is the purpose "know me better." He wasn't giving his audience anything to do, and they couldn't figure out how to appropriately connect to his story.

We dug a little and found out he volunteered in his son's facility and had become an advocate for involved parenthood. His relationship with his son was excellent now, and he was helping him gain an education in advance of his release. He had also started an advocacy group for parents in similar situations. Suddenly, he realized that by clearly showing how his personal, difficult story connected to a meaningful outcome, he could engage and move his audience.

Tom realized that by sharing the "so what" of his story, he gave people an anchor. His speech's action and purpose changed: he wanted to convince parents to be diligently involved in their children's lives and to perhaps even dedicate some of their volunteer time to parent-involvement advocacy. He wanted his example to both inspire people to action and raise awareness.

That information changed the entire room. His colleagues were able to let him know that by giving them an outcome that had meaning, they could relate to him and his work, be inspired by his story, and respect his experience. In other words, the presenter didn't leave the audience with the difficult question "What do I do with this information now?" He gave them a way to connect with his topic and use it. His classmates told him that if he had added those outcomes to the story, they would be inspired to seize every day and be great parents.

This is how great presenters use personal stories. They know the lesson they are teaching, and by entering into some vulnerability, they show the audience that they're human. As a result, their passion can then move people to action.

JACK, THE FAKER

I once saw a keynote speaker (Jack) at a conference of about nine hundred people. Jack's topic was, believe it or not, authenticity. He was funny in his opening, but he told us that he was going to get serious and very emotional with us later in his talk. I have to admit, my skeptical side popped up when he mentioned this. How did he know he would be emotional? It's okay, I figured, he'll probably have a really powerful story to share.

He pulled us through stories about honesty and the importance of integrity. And then it came—the story of losing his pet. Very sad, true, but guess what he did then? He faked tears. I was in the first row, and you cannot fake out an actor. I'd know a phony cry even from the back row, and this was it. I heard murmurs of sympathy from a few audience members, and I have to hand it to him, he was an excellent fraud. But I wasn't the only person he didn't fool. Most of the other executives sitting around me were rolling their eyes and wondering how much longer this was going to go on.

I was embarrassed. As a professional, Jack should have known better. As you may have guessed, I have endless patience for the foibles of anyone trying to become a better presenter. I have absolutely none for paid professionals who fake it. Forcing emotion to manipulate an outcome is wrong because you've stopped being authentic and have become an imposter—and that's exactly what we're trying to eradicate here.

Fake passion is bad passion. When you've stopped feeling it and are going through the motions, it's time to get off the stage.

MARC, THE LEADER

I've had the good fortune to work for one of the biggest packaged-food producers in the world. My company has provided executive presence and communication training for several of its research centers, which are innovative, interesting, and science-focused places. The head of one of those centers, Marc, was a charismatic leader. He was brought from overseas to run a US center, and he led it into a golden age during his tenure. The employees loved him, and his plans for continuous improvement were far-reaching and exciting. In addition, he mentioned to me that his family was happy here. Life was rockin' for Marc.

But right in the middle of this great work, the company decided to accelerate Marc's leadership plan. He'd always known that he was being groomed for higher-level responsibilities, but he'd been told they were several years away. The news was both a compliment and an unexpected twist. He had to manage a succession plan at work, move his family back overseas in the middle of the school year, and adjust to leaving a team he really enjoyed.

On his last day at the center, Marc gave a farewell speech. It was full of humor and stories, and he encouraged the team to embrace this change and continue to exceed company expectations. As he was telling his colleagues how much they meant to him, he choked up. This intelligent, charismatic, in-control leader lost it. Tears came to his eyes, and he had to stop speaking to get a hold of himself. He rubbed his nose, took a few breaths, and finally continued his speech. He finished beautifully, and the team applauded, many of them in tears as well.

When I spoke to him later, he confided that he was upset with himself for losing control of his emotions. He admitted that he hadn't realized just how strongly he felt about this change. He was suddenly sad when he stood up in front of those great people and had to say good-bye. I told him that his speech and his emotional reaction were both absolutely appropriate. He showed his genuine feelings about a very intense and unexpected situation. He let the emotion happen, took a minute to pull himself together, and continued on. What he didn't realize was that in that moment, he had authentically shared himself with his team. They were touched, moved, and even a bit relieved to see that their leader was just as upset about the change as they were.

Speaking to people at the center now, the story of Marc's farewell speech is practically legend. It's proof that even the highest levels of leadership care about them. That moment of emotion made Marc an even better leader in their eyes because of his humanity. That single moment of vulnerability connected him to them forever. It was important to the team—to know that they meant so much to a man who was moving on to bigger things.

NOW GET OUT THERE!

The CFO of a multibillion-dollar health-care company once addressed an internal group of young leaders. He talked about meetings and presentations to stockholders and how tough those could be. The best part of his speech, however, was how he embraced his badness. He talked about how his "bad presentations" were an asset to his career and company. You see, his delivery was not polished—it was down-to-earth, focused on the market, and extremely casual. He stood in stark contrast to the CEO, who was a consummate salesman, very energetic, and decidedly polished. The cool part was that they both realized that they made the perfect team. Stockholders need to hear about excitement and growth plans from a charismatic leader. But when it comes to the numbers and the tough questions, they want to hear it from someone who comes across as fair, honest, and approachable. For this guy, it was like a badge of honor—people trusted him more for his imperfection. He was being his bad self in the best way.

How about you? I hope your head is stuffed with all sorts of ideas from this book, and I hope you brazenly walk out and break a few rules. But more than anything, I hope you *do* something. It's great to read, consider, and discuss things, but until you do something, we may never know just how fabulously bad you can be.

Improv taught me to do stuff—even when I didn't know what to say, I would step out and start doing an action. I knew a troupe member would step up to fill the void, and action was always the most powerful choice.

So choose some low-risk venues to start practicing—a local

association, school, or book club. Come up with a ten-minute speech for them and try breaking some rules and strutting your stuff. If a few techniques work well, great. Try them again. Then you'll have them as part of your own authentic delivery and can use them in more important situations, like a committee presentation at work.

Make bold choices. Try lots of different things. Practice all sorts of wild openings and fabulous stories, do things you've never considered, and keep trying. You'll start becoming more and more comfortable with being your baddest you. Come on, people. Fists in the air, and shout it with me:

"I'm bad!"

"I'm really bad!"

"I'm the best bad presenter EVER!"

Now get out there and do it.

We are what we repeatedly do. Excellence therefore is not an act, but a habit.

—Aristotle

NOTES

Introduction: So Who Said You're A Bad Presenter?

1. Sally Hogshead, "How to Fascinate," in *The ASTD Management Development Handbook*, ed. Lisa Haneberg (Alexandria, VA: ASTD Press, 2012), 416.

One: The Baddest Way to Prepare—Start Breaking the Rules Before You Even Hit the Stage

1. David Rock and Jeffrey Schwartz, "The Neuroscience of Leadership: Breakthroughs in Brain Research Explain How to Make Organizational Transformation Succeed." *Strategy+Business* 43 (May 30, 2006), http://www.strategy-business.com/article/06207.

2. Malcolm Gladwell, *Outliers: The Story of Success* (New York: Little, Brown and Company, 2008).

3. Tony Schwartz, "The Way We're Working Isn't Working: More and More, Less and Less," in *The ASTD Management Development Handbook*, ed. Lisa Haneberg (Alexandria, VA: ASTD Press, 2012).

4. Joshua Foer, *Moonwalking with Einstein: The Art and Science of Remembering Everything* (New York: Penguin Books, 2012).

5. K. Ericsson, R. T. Krampe, and C. Tesch-Romer, "The Role of Deliberate Practice in the Acquisition of Expert Performance," *Psychological Review* 100, no. 3 (1993): 363–406.

6. Gladwell, *Outliers*, 50

7. Anne Lamott, *Bird by Bird: Some Instructions on Writing and Life* (New York: Anchor Books, 1994).

Two: You Are the Presentation—So Be Your Baddest You

1. Norman Miller and Donald T. Campbell, "Recency and Primacy in Persuasion as a Function of the Timing of Speeches and Measurements," *Journal of Abnormal and Social Psychology* 59, no. 1 (July 1959), 1–9.

2. Daniela Schiller et al., "A Neural Mechanism of First Impressions," *Nature Neuroscience* 12, no. 4 (April 2009): 508–14.

3. Paul J. Zak, "The Neurobiology of Trust," *Scientific American* (June 2008): 88–95.

4. *FDR: Selected Speeches of President Franklin D. Roosevelt* (St. Petersburg, FL: Red and Black Publishers, 2010), 135.

5. T. F. Cunningham, A. F. Healy, and D. M. Williams, "Effects of Repetition on Short-Term Retention of Order Information," *Journal of Experimental Psychology, Learning, Memory and Cognition* 10, no. 4 (October 1984): 575–97.

6. John F. Kennedy, quoted in Halford Ross Ryan, ed., *Inaugural Addresses of Twentieth-Century American Presidents* (Greenwood Publishing Group, 1993), 188.

7. Martin Luther King, quoted in Ed Clayton, *Martin Luther King: The Peaceful Warrior* (New York: Simon & Schuster, 1968).

8. Quoted in Vivian Buchan, *Make Presentations with Confidence* (Barron's Educational Series, 1997), 93.

9. Eric Finzi and Erika Wasserman, "Treatment of Depression with Botulinum Toxin A: A Case Series," *Dermatological Surgery* 32, no. 5 (May 2006): 645–50, http://www.drfinzi.com/Portals/0/docs/botox.pdf.

10. Dana R. Carney, Amy J. C. Cuddy, and Andy J. Yap, "Power Posing: Brief Nonverbal Displays Affect Neuroendocrine Levels and Risk Tolerance," *Psychological Science* 21, no. 10 (2010): 1363–68.

11. Julia Hanna, "Power Posing: Fake It Until You Make It," Harvard Business School, September 20, 2010, http://hbswk.hbs.edu/item/6461.html.

12. "Silent Messages" by Albert Mehrabian, 1980. Nonverbal Communication by Albert Mehrabian, 2007. Learn more about the study at Mehrabian's website, http://www.kaaj.com/psych/.

13. "Invisible Made Visible," *This American Life*, National Public Radio, episode 464, May 18, 2012, http://www.thisamericanlife.org/radio-archives/episode/464/invisible-made-visible.

14. "Quick Statistics," National Institute on Deafness and Other Communication Disorders, US Department of Health and Human Services, http://www.nidcd.nih.gov/health/statistics/Pages/quick.aspx.

15. Adapted from Ray Blunt, "Leaders and Stories: Growing the Next Generation, Conveying Values, and Shaping Character," http://govleaders.org/stories.htm.

16. Annie Murphy Paul, "Your Brain on Fiction," *New York Times Sunday Review*, March 17, 2012, http://www.nytimes.com/2012/03/18/opinion/sunday/the-neuroscience-of-your-brain-on-fiction.html?pagewanted=all&_r=2&.

17. Leo Widrich, "The Science of Storytelling: Why Telling a Story Is the

Most Powerful Way to Activate Our Brains," *LifeHacker*, December 5, 2012, http://lifehacker.com/5965703/the-science-of-storytelling-why-telling-a-story-is-the-most-powerful-way-to-activate-our-brains.

18. http://www.edwardtufte.com/bboard/q-and-a-fetch-msg?msg_id=0001OB.

19. Beth Dickey, "Safety Assessments Released on Four NASA projects," *Government Executive*, May 12, 2004, http://www.govexec.com/management/2004/05/safety-assessments-released-on-four-nasa-projects/16683/.

20. Denis L. Loyd et al., "Expertise in Your Midst: How Congruence Between Status and Speech Style Affects Reactions to Unique Knowledge," *Group Processes & Intergroup Relations* 13, no. 3 (2010): 379–95.

Three: Oops!—Staying Bad, No Matter What Happens

1. Gene Perrett, "Do and Don'ts for When the Mike Won't Work," *Toastmaster*, January 2006, 14, http://www.toastmasters.org/mainmenucategories/freeresources/needhelpgivingaspeech/tipstechniques/whenthingsgowrong.aspx.

2. Rosamund Stone Zander and Benjamin Zander, *The Art of Possibility: Transforming Professional and Personal Life* (New York: Penguin Books, 2000).

3. Andrew Weil, "Breathing: Three Exercises," http://www.drweil.com/drw/u/ART00521/three-breathing-exercises.html.

4. Daniel Goleman, Richard Boyatzis, and Annie McKee, *Primal Leadership: Learning to Lead with Emotional Intelligence* (Boston: Harvard Business Review Press, 2004).

Sources for Quotations

Robert Allen, http://www.quoteswave.com/picture-quotes/102144.

Maya Angelou, "A Conversation with Dr. Maya Angelou," by Trasha LaNae, *Beautifully Said Magazine* (July 4, 2012), http://beautifullysmagazine.com/201207feature-of-the-month-3.

Seve Ballesteros, www.quotesdaddy.com/author/Seve+Ballesteros.

Dale Carnegie, quoted in Eric Garner, *The Art of Communicating* (Ventus Publishing ApS, 2012).

Leonard Cohen, "Anthem." Copyrighted music, Sony/ATV Songs LLC, Stranger Music Inc., Shanna Crooks Songs, 1967.

David Cooperrider and Diana Whitney, *Appreciative Inquiry: A Positive Revolution in Change* (San Francisco: Berrett-Koehler, 2005).

Fortune cookie, acquired at Great Wall Kitchen, Brooklyn Heights, New York, http://www.menupages.com/restaurants/great-wall-7.

Judy Garland, m.imdb.com/name/nm0000023/quotes.

Malcolm Gladwell, *Outliers: The Story of Success* (New York: Little, Brown and Company, 2008), 42.

David Arthur Hough, Lake Kahola, Kansas. Spoken repeatedly during the summers of 1977–90.

Elbert Hubbard, quoted in Vivian Buchan, *Make Presentations with Confidence* (Barron's Educational Series, 1997), 43.

Ivan Lendl, http://www.brainyquote.com/quotes/authors/i/ivan_lendl.html?vm=1.

Seán O'Casey, www.goodreads.com/author/quotes/11582.Se_n_O_Casey.

Blaise Pascal, quoted in Fred R. Shapiro, ed. *The Yale Book of Quotations* (New Haven, CT: Yale University Press, 2006), 583.

Anna Quindlen, http://thinkexist.com/quotation/the-thing-that-is-really-hard-and-really-amazing/365647.html.

ACKNOWLEDGMENTS

I'd like to thank my family for supporting me through another book process—Todd, Timothy, Kate, Trey, Mom, Dad, Tom, Cathy, all the Kansas cousins, my Wyoming cousins, and my Columbus family. Special thanks to my editor, Neil Maillet, who came up with this idea in the first place. The incredible team at Berrett-Koehler, who are the finest professionals in the industry—Steve, Jeevan, Kirsten, Dianne, Michael, David, Katie, Kat, Charlotte, Bob, Kathy, Kylah, Seth, Richard, Zoe, Arielle, Johanna, Ginger, Courtney, Catherine, Maria, Anna. My amazing ImprovEdge ensemble—Lisa, Wonder Woman, Puma, Kitch, Zoe, Mr. Syrup Representative, Sudy, April, Melissa, Jamie, Shepperd, Michelle, Ramon, Erika, Doc, Dionysia, Clark, Kristie, Money Lady, Randy. My girlfriends who listened—Jane, Frances, Pat, Matina, Joanne, Nina, Anne, Tara. Thank you to my wonderful clients who cheered me on through the process and agreed to review and provide testimonials for the book. And thanks to all the people with whom I've worked and coached. I've learned more from you than any other source, and I thank you for your courage, stories, and energy. I'm so grateful to get to be here again.

INDEX

Karen Hough is the Amazon #1 best-selling author of *The Improvisation Edge: Secrets to Building Trust and Radical Collaboration at Work.* Her book also made the Top 25 Business Books on 800-CEO-READ. Karen is the founder and CEO of ImprovEdge, which creates corporate training using improvisation. ImprovEdge won the silver International Stevie Award for Most Innovative Company of the Year 2012 and has received the Athena PowerLink Award for outstanding woman-owned business. She is a regular contributor to The Huffington Post.

Karen's first life was as a professional improviser and actor. She trained with Chicago's Second City, performed in more than one hundred theatrical productions, and was featured in radio, TV, and film. She lived a second life as a successful executive in IT for network engineering start-ups. She finally became an entrepreneur. ImprovEdge has a presence in six cities nationwide and a client list that includes ESPN, JPMorgan, OhioHealth, Turner Broadcasting, Coach, and Nationwide Insurance, to name a few. Karen is a graduate of Yale University and La Sorbonne, Paris IV. She serves on several boards and is deeply committed to volunteer activities. Karen lives with her husband and three children in Ohio.

Also by Karen Hough

The Improvisation Edge

Secrets to Building Trust and Radical Collaboration at Work

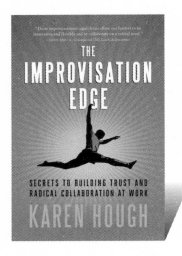

All kinds of books have been written about building trust and teamwork. But this is the only one that draws on the knowledge of experts in trust building: theatrical improvisers. Improvisers must create deep trust, collaborate radically, manage risk, and turn disasters into opportunities—which are also vital business skills. Karen Hough describes four secrets that help leaders, trainers, managers, and frontline employees adopt the improviser's mind-set. She offers a hands-on way to build an organizational culture that makes breakthrough business results possible.

"These improvisational capabilities allow our leaders to be innovative and flexible and to collaborate on a radical level."
   —**John Brock, Chairman and CEO, Coca-Cola Enterprises**

Paperback, 192 pages, ISBN 978-1-60509-585-1
PDF ebook, ISBN 978-1-60509-659-9

BK® Berrett–Koehler Publishers, Inc.
San Francisco, *www.bkconnection.com*   **800.929.2929**

Berrett–Koehler
Publishers

Berrett-Koehler is an independent publisher dedicated to an ambitious mission: *Creating a World That Works for All*.

We believe that to truly create a better world, action is needed at all levels—individual, organizational, and societal. At the individual level, our publications help people align their lives with their values and with their aspirations for a better world. At the organizational level, our publications promote progressive leadership and management practices, socially responsible approaches to business, and humane and effective organizations. At the societal level, our publications advance social and economic justice, shared prosperity, sustainability, and new solutions to national and global issues.

A major theme of our publications is "Opening Up New Space." Berrett-Koehler titles challenge conventional thinking, introduce new ideas, and foster positive change. Their common quest is changing the underlying beliefs, mindsets, institutions, and structures that keep generating the same cycles of problems, no matter who our leaders are or what improvement programs we adopt.

We strive to practice what we preach—to operate our publishing company in line with the ideas in our books. At the core of our approach is stewardship, which we define as a deep sense of responsibility to administer the company for the benefit of all of our "stakeholder" groups: authors, customers, employees, investors, service providers, and the communities and environment around us.

We are grateful to the thousands of readers, authors, and other friends of the company who consider themselves to be part of the "BK Community." We hope that you, too, will join us in our mission.

A BK Life Book

This book is part of our BK Life series. BK Life books change people's lives. They help individuals improve their lives in ways that are beneficial for the families, organizations, communities, nations, and world in which they live and work. To find out more, visit **www.bk-life.com**.

Berrett–Koehler
Publishers

A community dedicated to creating
a world that works for all

Dear Reader,

Thank you for picking up this book and joining our worldwide community of Berrett-Koehler readers. We share ideas that bring positive change into people's lives, organizations, and society.

To welcome you, we'd like to offer you a free e-book. You can pick from among twelve of our bestselling books by entering the promotional code **BKP92E** here: http://www.bkconnection.com/welcome.

When you claim your free e-book, we'll also send you a copy of our e-newsletter, the *BK Communiqué*. Although you're free to unsubscribe, there are many benefits to sticking around. In every issue of our newsletter you'll find

- A free e-book
- Tips from famous authors
- Discounts on spotlight titles
- Hilarious insider publishing news
- A chance to win a prize for answering a riddle

Best of all, our readers tell us, "Your newsletter is the only one I actually read." So claim your gift today, and please stay in touch!

Sincerely,

Charlotte Ashlock
Steward of the BK Website

Questions? Comments? Contact me at bkcommunity@bkpub.com.

MIX
Paper from
responsible sources
FSC® C005010

Certified

Corporation
bcorporation.net